To Christine
It was wonderfu[l]
about your jo[urney]

M. Paula Duons[?]

Christine, I'm looking forward
to merging our spiritual
experiences. I'm so delighted
to get to know you.

Evelyn Hurlock

JOLT

MapleWheat Publications

JOLT:
Engaged and On Target

M. Paula Daoust, Ph.D.
Evelyn I. Eubank

MapleWheat Publishing

Topeka, Kansas

MapleWheat Publishing
3420 SE Hackberry Ct.
Topeka, KS 66605
785.267.3505
To order visit: http://www.MomentumBusinessGroup.com

ISBN: 0-9778955-0-5

Printed in the United States of America

Cover Design by Libby Tidwell

MapleWheat Publishing   First Edition

Dedicated to Dan and Steve

Without your support and lifelong friendship,
this wouldn't have happened.

Table of Contents

Appendices

Assessment Tools

Chapter 1

Prospering in a Hostile World

"The alternative is not between change or no change, but
between change for the better or change for the worse."
Clifford Hugh Douglas

Potiphar Breen, a character in Robert Heinlein's classic sci-fi story, *The Year of the Jackpot,* curiously tracked the patterns of seemingly random events. Fascinated by the cyclical nature of the data, he noticed that occasionally the cycles of two or three variables would coincide, changing together like a dance, before separating to continue their own unique patterns. Then one day, all of the variables converged and, when that occurred, the universe collapsed.

Change is occurring at a rate never seen before in the history of man. Behavior that was effective in slower, more stable times no longer works well in today's business climate. Like Breen, you can pas-

sively monitor the changes. Worse yet, you can ig-
nore that change is accelerating. In either case, the
universe will probably not collapse as it did for
Breen, but on a personal level, it might feel as though
it did. There is another alternative available; you can
choose to use these changes to help you *thrive* in
hostile times.

Change is no longer negotiable. Managers and organizations that understand this are making adjustments that are giving them a competitive edge. Like
a sailboat captures the wind, these organizations are
not just surviving change, they are harnessing its
energy to get where they want to go. These managers and organizations are engaged and on-target to
success and you can be too,

Your organization can do more than survive change, it can thrive on it!

if you decide to take effective action. Your organization can do more than survive change; it can thrive
on it! The choice is yours.

Derrick and Gerald are two managers who were
hired two years ago to supervise similar departments
in different companies of a similar size, in a similar
market. Unfortunately, they have not enjoyed the
same success in their new positions. When Derrick
signed on, he was enthusiastic about his new job and
optimistic about his future with his new employer.
Derrick understood that promotions depended on
doing more than just meeting expectations. To get
to the next level, Derrick believed he needed to produce exceptional results. When Derrick took the
job, he knew that he could produce those exceptional results but, two years later, he is having big
doubts. Some days he feels like things are stacked

against him. As with many other companies, Derrick is running his department with fewer staff than last year but the pace and quantity of work have increased. His staff are stressed, cooperation between departments and even within his own staff is poor and conflict is frequent. Running around putting out fires has chewed up any "think-time," so planning ahead just isn't happening. There was a time Derrick enjoyed his job, but lately, it's hard to get up in the morning.

Gerald started a new job about the same time as Derrick but things are a lot different for him. He began the new job with the same enthusiasm and confidence as Derrick but, two years later, Gerald still loves his job. Most days he can't wait to get to the office. He feels valued and is proud of the work his staff produces. He and his staff work hard but they also enjoy being together and they have fun. Gerald is getting the results he expected and knows his future is bright.

Why is Gerald's experience so different from Derrick's? The easy answer to this is that Gerald is a better manager than Derrick, but that is like saying, "Jenny's sick because she has a fever." What *makes* the difference? Both Gerald and Derrick started their new jobs expecting to do well. So, what happened? How did Gerald become a star performer and Derrick slip to, at best, adequate? Was Derrick somehow inferior in skill or personality to Gerald? Does the fault lie with Derrick's supervisor? Did Derrick not get the same quality of coaching and direction that Gerald got? Maybe the problem is not with Derrick or his supervisor; maybe Derrick's organization is the critical factor. Is there something inherently different about Gerald's organization that made it easier for him to be successful? Derrick, his supervisor, and his organization all had a vested interest in Derrick being successful. So, why did Derrick move from being enthusiastic and confident to becoming disillusioned and frustrated?

If your work experience is more like Derrick's than Gerald's, you may be thinking that someone like Gerald doesn't exist. However, people like Gerald do exist. The key to their success is simple. It's called engagement. Gerald is engaged in his work and Derrick is becoming *un*engaged.

With work engagement, productivity and morale go hand-in-hand. If you are working with folks who are unengaged like Derrick, and you want to change things, then you will want to increase engagement in yourself and those around you.

That's what *JOLT* is about: creating great places to work so that engagement can flourish. The chapters that follow will give you the tools to boost the energy within and around you so that you can produce exceptional results. You will simultaneously increase productivity AND morale. And, you will energize your career and your organization and put them both on target to success!

Work Engagement occurs when employees' values, beliefs and goals are aligned with the purpose of the organization such that they are personally committed to contributing to the accomplishment of the organization's mission.

Work Engagement

The critical difference between Gerald and Derrick is that Gerald is engaged and Derrick is not. How did this happen when they both began their new jobs with high engagement? Their work environments are very different. Gerald works with people who are like him and are highly engaged. Derrick works with people who are stressed and unhappy. One environment is able to create, maintain and enhance engagement, the other cannot. That is a big difference.

Work engagement is "working on purpose!"

Work engagement means that a person is "working on purpose." He or she is deliberately *choosing* to do more than is required. The person is making this choice because the work has purpose, it is personally meaningful. Work engagement occurs when employees' values, beliefs and goals are aligned with those of the organization such that they are ***personally committed*** to contributing to the accomplishment of the organization's mission.

The definition of work engagement varies between authors but all of the definitions share this perspective -- when an employee is engaged, his or her own personal goals are aligned with the organization's goals. When an employee is engaged, the employee willingly does more than is absolutely required by the job. The individual does so because helping the organization achieve its goals simultaneously helps the individual achieve his or her own goals. The individual and the organization are connected.

Other Definitions of Engagement

- *...the degree to which people come to work every day with a compelling, active, and passionate interest in their work (Herman, Olivo & Gioia, 2003)*

- *...the degree to which individuals are personally committed to helping an organization by doing a better job than required to hold the job (Kowalski, 2002)*

- *...employees...who work longer hours, try harder, accomplish more and speak positively about their organizations (Wellins & Concelman, 2005)*

- *...highly motivated and capable [employees] performing the activities that drive organizational success (Bernthal, 2004a)*

- *...employees...who find personal meaning and motivation in their work (Bernthal, 2004b)*

- *To be fully engaged, we must be physically energized, emotionally connected, mentally focused and spiritually aligned with a purpose beyond our immediate self-interest (Loehr & Schwartz, 2005).*

Work engagement is important to an organization because engaged employees don't just meet their goals, they *exceed* them! The effect of increasing engagement on organizations has been well researched. The results can be summarized in one statement: If you improve the overall level of engagement in your organization, just about every other positive change you are targeting will also improve. For example, in a study Clifton did for Gallup, he reported that engaged employees were responsible for all customer satisfaction their corporation enjoyed and they were the drivers of the company's financial success. (2004)

Since an engaged employee is committed to the organization's success, it is reasonable to conclude that this employee would be less likely to leave, less likely to be absent from work, more likely to be productive and more likely to attend to issues related to quality control and customer satisfaction. Study after study demonstrates that increasing an organization's level of overall engagement results in corresponding increases in important organizational results. It is in an organization's best interests to cultivate engagement in its employees.

The reality is, however, that engaged employees are the exception, not the rule. Gallup's national representative survey of employed adults found that only 26% of the American workforce was engaged (Gal-

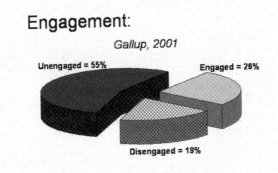

Engagement:

Gallup, 2001

Unengaged = 55%   Engaged = 26%

Disengaged = 19%

lup, 2001a). The rest of the population was either unengaged or disengaged. Unengaged employees are discouraged and unwilling to do more than is required to maintain their employment. Disengaged employees are are a different matter. They are angry with the organization and are actively working against the organization's success and goals. Derrick was unengaged, not disengaged. He was frustrated and discouraged but he still wanted to do the right thing for his organization. If the organization made the right changes, Derrick could easily become engaged again. That's good news!

Studies Show that When Engagement Improves:

↑ profitability
↑ sales
↑ earnings per
   employee
↑ retention
↑ productivity
↑ client satisfaction
↑ staff satisfaction
↑ quality
↑ innovation
↑ initiative
↑ teamwork
↑ accuracy

↓ absenteeism
↓ Worker's Comp.
   claims
↓ grievances
↓ tardiness
↓ conflict between
   employees
↓ off-task behavior
↓ turnover
↓ theft by employees
↓ serious illness
   amongst employees

If 74% of the population is unengaged or disengaged, only one in four employees is like Gerald and these employees are not evenly dispersed throughout the workforce. Rather, they are more likely to occur in groups. Unless you happen to be engaged, it is quite likely that, except for a new employee, you have not worked with anyone else who is engaged! The sad fact is that, according to the Gallup (2005) study, although many new employees begin their jobs engaged, six months later only 38% are still engaged and this drops to 22% by the end of the third year. What is making it so difficult to create and maintain engagement?

21st Century Challenges

Most organizations are being overwhelmed with the rate and range of change. The result is they have become reactive, dealing with whatever crisis is most threatening. Working in environments like this, even the most optimistic personality will get worn down over time. When an organization is responding to change-induced crises instead of planning for change, important-but-not-urgent issues are not addressed. Over time, the organization's resources, including the work engagement of employees, deteriorates.

What are the major variables in today's work environment that are putting such stress on organizations? In a nutshell, they are related to:

- Economic downturn
- Technology development

- Increasing global competition
- Generational differences in the workplace
- Changes in immigration policy

An economic downturn:

When the economy slows, the knee-jerk reaction of organizations is to cut staffing costs. Lorne's company was no different. Profits were down and the company first cut the "frills." The on-site daycare was closed and the exercise facility was converted to office space. Merit increases were not offered and soon after that, layoffs began.

Lorne survived the first round of layoffs but that has been a mixed blessing because he has had to take on a lot more work. He's so tired and frustrated that even when he works late and cuts corners on quality, he still can't get it all done. Being creative or taking a risk is no longer an option. Doing what it takes to hold onto the job is his focus now. In the meantime, he'll keep an eye out for something better with another company.

Technology development:

The rapid rate of technological advancement has revolutionized work. Tim works for a manufacturing company that used to employ many labor-intensive entry-level positions. The plant has been re-engineered and almost all of those positions have disappeared. Now, fewer people are needed but those that are needed require more technical expertise and they are scarce.

Tim used to hire high school graduates but now

even college graduates need extensive training after they are hired. His company worked with the local college but adjusting the curriculum to reflect the changes in technology was like aiming at a moving target. As a result, Tim is now relying on employees to do some independent study or he is using the company's training department to upgrade skills. Sending people to training creates staff shortages that his work group has to absorb. Adding to the frustration, once someone is properly trained, the new skills are highly marketable and Tim often loses the employee to other companies.

Increasing global competition:

As a result of technological advances, the business world has become smaller. Off-shore international corporations now compete successfully with American corporations in a variety of industries ranging from manufacturing to support services. More recently the trend has even been extended to include professional services such as engineering and medical care.

Glenda works for a software company and she has been watching the trends carefully. If her company has to compete with the off-shore international corporations on price, she knows that it won't survive. The challenge for her is to help her staff understand that the only way the company will be able to continue to compete is if it can provide better quality, be more innovative or be able to complete projects more quickly than an off-shore company. Convincing her staff isn't an easy task. They feel the pressure to produce more but the company isn't offering anything in return for the extra effort except continued employment. That doesn't look like a fair deal to her staff.

Sam Walton said, "It takes two weeks for an employee to treat customers the way he is being treated." How staff are treated is reflected in their work. If they are feeling that the company doesn't care about them, they aren't going to feel very motivated to provide the quality, innovation, customer service and productivity that will be needed to be competitive with global competition.

Generational differences in the workplace:

The workplace now includes four generations of workers: the Veterans, Boomers, Y-generation and the X'rs (who are often called Nexters). With the flattening of organizational hierarchies and increased reliance on technology, the generations are working more closely together than in previous eras. The education and cultural experience of the groups is very different and as a result, their approach to work is also different.

Eve supervises the business office of a large legal firm. She started out as a receptionist 25 years ago and is very proud of the position she now holds. She works hard and when there is an important deadline, she willingly works overtime. Her family is important to her but she believes that sometimes you just have to make sacrifices.

In the last few years, Eve has been frustrated with several of the younger staff she hired. They don't seem to have the same commitment she had when she started her career. They don't stay with the firm very long so she has had to spend a lot of time hiring and training. They also expect a lot more feedback than Eve is used to giving, which is another drain on her time. When overtime is needed, the younger staff resist staying late. The thing that is hardest for Eve is that these young employees expect to make decisions and be in charge of any project in which they are involved. It seems to Eve that they aren't willing to do their time in the trenches like everyone else has done. Instead, the young employees expect to jump right in at the top of the ladder. Eve is disappointed with what she perceives as a lack of work ethic but she also suspects that several of her younger staff think she is unreasonable.

"The children now love luxury; they have bad manners, contempt for authority; they show disrespect for elders and love chatter in place of exercise. Children are now tyrants, not the servants of their households. They no longer rise when elders enter the room. They contradict their parents, chatter before company, gobble up dainties at the table, cross their legs, and tyrannize their teachers."

Socrates as quoted by Plato

Changes in immigration policy:

In the past, the United States has proudly described itself as a "nation of immigrants." The economy was helped with the skills and training many immigrants brought with them. Many American companies relied on immigrants who had the technological skills necessary to fill key positions. But with the fear of terrorism and the tightening of borders, immigration has been slowed and jobs are remaining empty.

Adam is the Director of the Human Resource department of a large engineering company. His company has always preferred hiring Americans but when they didn't get qualified applicants, they used to fill positions by sponsoring the immigration of a good candidate. Asian countries were often good sources of well-educated and highly qualified candidates. Since 9-11, however, immigration from anywhere has become more difficult and it is particularly difficult from countries that are considered a potential terrorist threat. The result for Adam's company is that positions that require a high degree of technical skill can sometimes be unfilled for months and months, which cripples the company's ability to bid on new contracts or complete critical jobs according to agreed timelines.

Heinlein's story, *The Year of the Jackpot*, has some relevance to today's business environment. Unlike Breen who very carefully monitored trends around him, many organizations are not monitoring the convergence of the five issues listed on pages 9-10. Instead they are attempting to respond to each issue as though it was occurring in isolation.

Your organization can make adjustments to any of these five issues individually and do fine. If two or three issues occurred together, your organization would have to be more strategic in its adjustments, but it can be done and the organization will continue to thrive. But, when most or all of these factors simultaneously peak, there is the risk that the organization will collapse, just as Breen's world collapsed.

Tipping

As if these factors are not enough, there is one more coming that will tip *the five issues over the top, making the pressure on your organization potentially overwhelming.*

It has been projected that by 2012 there will be 10 million more jobs in the American economy than there are people to fill them. This labor shortage is being caused by the aging of the "Baby Boomers" (people born between 1946 and 1964) and their subsequent exit from the labor force.

A further complication is that this projected shortage describes numbers only. Increasingly, unskilled labor jobs are disappearing. The jobs of today's labor market are skilled positions. Not everyone available to work will have the right training to fill the positions that are empty.

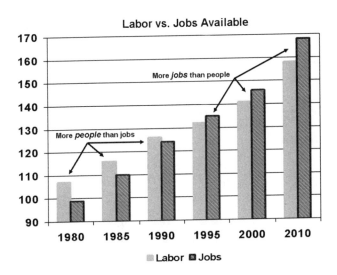

Labor vs. Jobs Available

What this graph shows is that in 1995 we passed the point where there are more positions to be filled than there are people to fill them. The slow down of the economy in 2000 masked this situation so your organization may not have noticed it. Not all organizations were protected, however. Some highly skilled positions have already felt the effect of shortages. *The Washington Post* recently described a situation in Maryland in which 7,500 skilled construction jobs were unfilled because qualified applicants could not be found. This was occurring while the labor force participation rate for the area was dropping! This is just a taste of what is yet to come.

You can use the energy produced by changes to propel yourself to your destination. The answer lies in engagement.

As more boomers choose to retire or, for health reasons, scale back their hours, the problem will become urgent. Your ability to keep your organization properly supplied with a labor force will become increasingly difficult. Positions will be open longer, you will have to compete more aggressively for good people and "head-hunters" will be stealing people away. The problem is of such magnitude that it will undoubtedly affect your business, even if the economy is not booming.

At a time when your organization needs to be making adjustments to deal with the first five issues that are eroding productivity and depleting engagement, the availability of people with the needed skills and experience is going to be shrinking. A serious consequence of running with lean numbers of employees is that there is no time for developing the workforce.

As a result, when the boomers leave, replacements from within the organization will, in most cases, not be prepared to step in.

It will also be difficult to find people outside the organization who can fill the competency void left by the boomers (Herman, et. al., 2003). Schools are not turning these folks out and immigration is unlikely to bring in the numbers necessary to make a significant difference to the gap. If an organization *does* manage to attract the right people, it may still have a problem. It will have a difficult time holding on to good people if management continues using outdated supervisory styles that were effective with the "boomers" but are counter-productive with a younger workforce (Branham, 2005; Herman, et. al., 2003).

So what is the answer? You can risk being capsized by these multiple waves and winds of change, or you can use the energy produced by these changes to propel yourself toward your destination. The answer lies in engagement and equipping yourself and your organization to compete and excel in this new labor market.

Excelling in the New Labor Market

The new labor market is a different kind of problem. Changing demographics in the workforce could be managed if that was the only change. So could the issue of rapidly changing technology with its accompanying changes in work competencies. Increased global competition has been dealt with in some form in the past, and the political nature of immigration polices has always existed. The same

New kinds of challenges require new solutions. can be said for the generational differences in work ethics. You only need to remember the quote Plato attributed to Socrates about the behavior of the younger generation to be reminded that each generation has trouble understanding the next. None of these issues are particularly new historically. It is the fact that all of these issues are occurring simultaneously that presents a new challenge of such magnitude that it threatens to overwhelm the unprepared organization.

New kinds of challenges require new solutions. Old answers won't work because old answers address one wave in isolation, not multiple waves.

The new paradigm must include intentional growth in engagement. Collaboration between all members of the organization is necessary. A major change will be in an overhaul of attitude towards employees. "Our employees are our best asset" has become such a common statement, that instead of inspiring and motivating employees, it has become a cliché.

An example of this cliché is Whitney's experience. She worked for an organization that professed to value its employees. Posted in the main lobby of the building was a nicely framed statement of the organization's core values. Neatly crossed out by a disgruntled employee were the statements, "Our employees are our most valuable resource" and "Our work environment will motivate people and encourage them to be productive." Amazingly, no one took the sign down after it was "modified."

Despite posting signs and making statements that the organization values its employees, most organizations don't really get it. The words are just words and they have not been integrated into the core of the organization's strategy. Covey (1990) says that employees are not important to a business; they ARE the business.

Without people, the machines don't run, sales aren't made and services aren't delivered. A paradigm shift is needed if an organization wants to excel. It won't be enough to "value" employees. To excel, the successful organization will focus on its employees *as its competitive edge.*

Engagement is the key to success in this new environment. Where high engagement occurs, great results follow for the organization. Most importantly, organizations with high engagement are great places to work. People don't often leave and when there is a position to be filled, there are plenty of applicants. While your competitors are struggling to survive, your organization can be running with energized, creative, and enthusiastic people. For your organization, there will NOT be a shortage of talent. Building an environment in which engagement flourishes will ensure that you always have the talent you need.

To create your great place to work you will need to build the conditions in which engagement can flourish. You will need targeted analysis and specific actions to maximize results. While it is possible to engineer high engagement for yourself, your workgroup or for your entire organization, it is unlikely to occur by accident.

The unique tools provided in the following chapters will allow you to diagnose your personal needs, the needs of your work group and the needs of your organization. Simple but comprehensive diagnostic metrics replace "trial and error" and "one-size-fits-all" attempts at improving engagement. Instead, you will have a targeted approach to identifying the key strategies that will get the performance improvement results you need. The tools and strategies described in the following chapters will put you on the leading edge of increasing productivity and morale.

Productivity without morale or, morale without productivity, cannot be sustained in the face of the multiple waves. But, when you increase both by focusing on engagement, you can put yourself into fast forward, moving to a new and higher level of operation. Instead of being overwhelmed by the multiple waves of change, you can seize the energy around you and prosper.

"A leader's role is to raise people's aspirations
for what they can become and to release their energies
so they will try to get there."
                                                          David Gergen

Chapter 2

The Co-generating System

"Synergy: With the right combination, one and one is much more than two!"

There are two major systems involved in creating energy to run a car: an electrical system and an internal combustion engine. In a traditional vehicle, the transmission is powered by an internal combustion engine but this process begins with electrical system igniting the gasoline. The engine system is dominant but requires the electrical system for support. In a hybrid vehicle, electricity powers the transmission with the gasoline engine providing extra power for bursts of speed. It is also the internal combustion engine that feeds the car with electrical energy by continually recharging the battery. The electrical system cannot function without its partnership with the traditional combustion system, creating a seamless, efficient, largely renewable resource!

The Co-generating System for creating organizational momentum offers you a similar vehicle for increasing both productivity and morale. The traditional approach to improving organizational effectiveness has been to emphasize increased productivity. This is like the combustion engine and has a similar effect. Continually putting pressure on a workforce to increase its production will have the effect of burning it out or alienating it. This approach will, as Covey (1995) describes, "kill the goose that lays the golden egg."

The Co-generating System offers a hybrid alternative by emphasizing improvements in engagement, which then improves productivity AND morale. In-

Co-generating Productivity and Engagement through the *Power of Three*

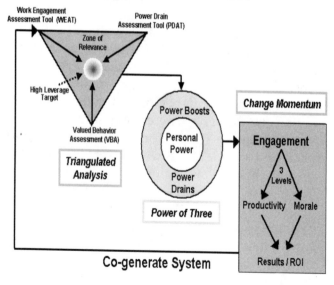

stead of depleting the system by emphasizing productivity, focus on increasing engagement regenerates the system. Like the car that uses two energy sources, a system that focuses on engagement will co-generate productivity *and* morale. It will increase organizational results in a powerful new way.

A key to co-generating productivity *and* engagement is addressing issues at the individual, group/work environment and organizational strategic/cultural levels. By targeting all three levels of an organization, the Co-generation System creates the Power of Three: Decrease in Power Drains, Power Boosts and Personal Power. Added to the Power of Three is Triangulated Analysis, which is a system for targeted strategy development and implementation. At all three levels, critical metrics are gathered to determine targets for action that will maximize the probability of success. The results of the change effort are measured continuously. Based on these results, adjustments are made to maximize engagement which then improves productivity and morale.

Overview of the Co-generating System

The following chapters of JOLT will describe the Co-generating System which is fueled by the Power of Three:
- *Power Drains,*
- *Power Boosts and*
- *Personal Power.*

JOLT explains how to pinpoint and improve those

workplace situations that "suck your will to live." Chapter 3 explains the Triangulated Analysis approach to identifying the most effective leverage points for improving organizational engagement.

Chapter 4 defines Power Drains and identifies the more common ones. It provides both a tool for identifying which Power Drains are most troublesome in your work environment. Suggested actions for reducing specific Power Drains are outlined in Appendix III. Reducing Power Drains will allow you to use the energy you produce for positive outcomes instead of wasting it through leakage. It will be easier to focus on the work and feel good about what you are doing when drains have been plugged.

On an organizational strategic/cultural level, JOLT explains ways to jumpstart your organization by creating Power Boosts. Chapter 5 addresses this second component of the Power of Three. The strategies for creating Power Boosts are described and tools for implementing them are provided. Carefully selected Power Boosts will magnify energy by aligning personal agendas with organizational goals.

JOLT provides a blueprint you can use to become more engaged on a personal level. Chapter 6 focuses on Personal Power, which consists of ten avenues for making changes in your own work experience. Each of the ten avenues offers several tools. You can choose which tools most suit your needs and build an individualized plan for increasing your personal power. A tool for identifying which avenues will be best suited to your needs is included

Jolt provides a blueprint for building engagement.

in this chapter. Strategies associated with each avenue are outlined in Appendix IV. You can also use these avenues to help your staff take more responsibility for their future by improving their own personal power. Using a combination of these avenues and the strategies associated with them will immediately improve the quality of your current work life and open new possibilities for future work.

Chapter 7 pulls the individual components together. By themselves each of the components - Power Drains, Power Boosts and Personal Power - make a significant difference in an organization. When all three are combined, you access the Power of Three and synergy emerges. Chapter 7 explains how to maximize this synergy by creating targeted strategies based on precise and accurate metrics. A unique feature of JOLT is its emphasis on demonstrating results. Once you have done the work of making changes, Chapter 7 of JOLT will provide you with some simple, easy-to-use tools to measure your results in terms of bottom-line dollars. When you explain the changes you have made to colleagues, your supervisor or senior management, you will not have to rely on opinion. Instead, you can provide objective data, translated to bottom-line dollar benefits, to support your claims.

"You are only as big as your dreams."
Luis Villalobos

Chapter 3

Measurement

"True genius resides in the capacity for evaluation of uncertain, hazardous, and conflicting information. "
Winston Churchill

Terrance recently announced to his staff a new initiative. The Vice President of HR had heard about work engagement and believed that it could help the organization. Terrance's staff rolled their eyes at the announcement. Bob murmured, just loud enough for Terrance to hear, "Flavor of the day." Terrance couldn't blame them. In the last five years there had been a number of initiatives and although a lot of effort had gone into them, not much had changed. Terrance didn't want to be negative but it did seem that these initiatives got in the way of getting work done. He couldn't honestly identify what problem these past initiatives were supposed to be fixing or what lasting benefit had come from them.

Terrance's experience is unfortunately a common one. Many organizations have implemented a variety of interventions that have yielded short-term, unmeasurable or no change. Credibility for organizational change is often low and frequently described as Bob did, "flavor of the day." This is not a surprising outcome when an organization repeatedly introduces a "fix" for a problem without doing the proper pre-work. The first phase of the Co-generating System for creating organizational change is a focused assessment, the Triangulated Analysis. A Triangulated Analysis will provide three angles with which to view the organization and this will help the organization avoid wasting time and precious resources making unnecessary changes with no real punch.

Triangulated Analysis involves understanding engagement from three perspectives. The first perspective the current engagement of employees. This is an essential beginning because it provides the baseline from which future meaurement can be compared. The second perspective involves scanning the environment to determine whether certain factors are present and, if so, what impact they have on the engagement level. The third perspective is an exploration of the behaviors that are most valued and reinforced by the work group.

Using these three perspectives for understanding the current condition of work engagement in an organization goes well beyond identification of the overall level of work engagement. They provide comprehensive information re-

Triangulated Analysis:
Three tools are used to understand the situation from three different angles.
- *Current Engagement*
- *Environmental Scan*
- *Valued Behaviors*

garding what particular factors are contributing to and detracting from work engagement in the organization. With this information, the organization can be efficient and effective in its effort to create a preferred working environment by focusing on high leverage targets for organizational change. Terrance's staff would therefore experience a minimum of disruption or distraction while sustainable, meaningful change is created. That is a very different approach and is built on using the three tools to *triangulate* the data.

Triangulating data means that you use three different tools with three different perspectives to view the organization. Each perspective individually provides clues regarding what issues are relevant and how engagement can be enhanced. When viewed from multiple angles, understanding is deepened in the same way as going from a two-dimensional

Model of Triangulate Analysis:

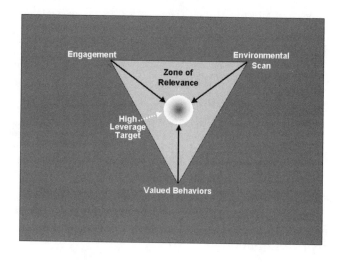

picture to a three-dimensional sculpture. The over-lapping of relevant issues from the multiple angles zeros in on a specific target that provides the most leverage for change.

Engagement

The concept of engagement emerged as a result of dissatisfaction with two older, familiar organizational development concepts:

a) staff or job satisfaction and
b) staff motivation.

Staff or job satisfaction has an interesting history. Likert, father of the popular Likert scales used in survey measurement, argued at the turn of the century that if working conditions were improved, productivity would also improve. Unfortunately, his efforts to provide evidence of this relationship failed but this is not a well known fact. It is logical that staff or job satisfaction should positively correlate with productivity and so, based on this simple face validity and Likert's reputation, the argument for improving staff or job satisfaction has been generally accepted in the business world.

It is not a well known fact that research has NEVER demonstrated that increasing job satisfaction will increase productivity!

Likert's work has resulted in the development of a wealth of commercial and organization-specific instruments for measuring staff or job satisfaction. Along with the instruments, a rich literature describing strategies for improving staff or job satisfaction has also emerged. Despite the interest and popularity of staff or job satisfaction as a target for organizational change, no one has ever succeeded in providing the evidence that eluded Likert!

Increasing staff or job satisfaction does not necessarily increase productivity. If you think about the issue you can easily think of circumstances in which a person could be very satisfied with his or her job but not be very productive. Simon loves his job because his supervisor doesn't care what he does with his time as long as he "looks" busy. Simon surfs the internet, takes care of personal business and keeps up with his buddies through email and online chats. Occasionally he fits in a little real work. Simon scores very high on the company's job satisfaction survey but he isn't very productive! While Simon may not be very productive, he is also unlikely to become violent at work. That is a very good thing but his organization needs more and is paying him to do more than just "look busy."

Motivation:
The psychological feature that arouses an organism to action toward a desired goal; the reason for an action.

Motivation is the other side of the coin. Staff or job satisfaction emphasizes the happiness of the employee. Motivation seeks to create conditions that encourage the employee to be more productive. It seeks to provide the employee with a reason to perform. There are just two ways to increase motivation: through inducements and by using incentives.

Inducements "make" people comply through threats

or actual punishment. Incentives involve manipulating rewards so that the employee "wants" to perform. In either case, the focus of motivation is to create conditions such that the employer maximizes the performance of employees. This is the "carrot and stick" approach. If you do well, you get the carrot. If you don't do well, you get the stick. In either case, you "get it."

If you go to Google or Amazon.com on the Internet and search using the term "motivation," you will find an overwhelming number of books, websites and articles offering advice on how staff motivation can be increased. The problem with the motivation literature is that it tends to be one-sided. Its focus is on creating benefits for the organization only. Benefits to the individual may occur but they are incidental to the primary objective of improving the organization. Gains in productivity made this way will last only as long as fear of the inducement or desire for the incentive exists. This is a challenge to maintain over time!

*Work Engagement increases staff **morale** AND it increases **productivity.** It is a win-win for the employee and the employer.*

Work engagement is built on both staff or job satisfaction AND motivation. Because it emphasizes both, it creates a win-win. Increases in staff morale AND increases in productivity occur together. Goals for both sides of the partnership, the employee and the employer, are of equal importance. Because both sides benefit, there is an incentive for both the employee and the employer to sustain the positive changes over time.

Indicators of Engagement

To be engaged means to be attracted to something
or have your attention held by something. If you
are engaged you are drawn into something and involved by it. This level of engagement is created by
a combination of personal interest and the opportunity to satisfy certain basic psychological needs such
as feeling connected to others, making a difference
in the world, or overcoming obstacles. These psychological needs are captured in the six pillars that
support work engagement:

- *Organizational Affinity:*
  This describes the degree to which an individual
  feels connected to, a part of, or loyal to the organization. It is a reflection of the degree of trust an
  individual feels toward the organization.

- *Recognition:*
  This is the degree to which an individual believes the organization values his or her individual contribution.

- *Job Match:*
  This is the degree to which an individual feels
  that the work uses his or her strengths and he or
  she enjoys the actual work.

- *Relationships:*
  This indicates how supported the individual
  feels by other people in the work environment.
  It is the degree to which an individual's social
  needs are met at work.

- *Growth/Challenge:*
  The degree to which an individual experiences challenge and opportunities to learn. This includes the degree to which the individual is able to use current skills in new ways, learn new skills or participate in new projects.

- *Empowerment:*
  This refers to an individual's perception of control and influence over issues that affect his or her work. It is the degree of decision-making an individual experiences in the job.

When work engagement is measured, the total score will be interesting but it is the score on these six indicators that will be most useful. The pattern of scores will identify organizational strengths. It will also identify where effort will provide the most positive change. These six indicator scores tell "the rest of the story." They help the investigator pull the curtain back to see what is happening backstage, out of view and most importantly, what is not happening that should be happening.

Assessing Work Engagement

You have several options for measuring work engagement. Many organizations have chosen to hire Gallup Consulting to conduct an assessment of the engagement of their employees using the Gallup *Q-12*. This is the pioneer tool and

WEAT Indicators

- *Organizational Affinity*
- *Recognition*
- *Job Match*
- *Relationships*
- *Growth/Challenge*
- *Empowerment*

consists of only twelve questions. The advantage of limiting the tool to a small number of questions is that it can be completed quickly. A risk with longer tools is that the respondent gets bored or tired and answers later questions in a haphazard manner. Another risk is that the respondent takes one look at the length of the tool and decides not to complete it at all. When doing research on attitudes, more is not necessarily better. The instrument needs to be sufficiently long to adequately sample the concept domain but not so long that it creates fatigue.

In addition to Gallup, there are other consulting firms that also have engagement assessment tools. They would also be willing to help you measure your organization's engagement.

Another way to get a tool to measure your organization's engagement would be to surf the Internet. If you do this, be sure to check whether the tool has published data to demonstrate its reliability and validity. Without this assurance, you may be using a tool that provides suspect results. If you base any decisions on unreliable or invalid data, both you and your organization could, at the very least, be wasting prescious resources on change efforts that were doomed at the outset. One other thing to keep in mind is that you will want to be sure that you are not violating any copyrights with whatever tool you choose to use to measure engagement.

A final option for assessing the work engagement of your workforce would be to use the Momentum Business Group's *Work Engagement Assessment Tool (WEAT)*. Like the Gallup *Q12*, The WEAT is a brief assessment, consisting of only thirty questions. This means that it can be completed in just a few minutes, which avoids the potential fatigue or boredom factor discussed earlier. The WEAT offers an advantage in that in addition to the overall global score, it also provides a score for the six indicators of engagement. This information will provide you with the first level of clues regarding what needs to start happening, stop happening or what needs to happen more frequently if work engagement is to improve in the organization. In addition to the six indicators, the WEAT expands the original three categories of disengaged, unengaged, and disengaged (discussed in Chapter 1) into six levels, two levels for each category. This provides a better understanding regarding the urgency for intervention or strengths of the workforce. For more information regarding the WEAT, see Appendix I.

Environmental Scan

The second tool in the Triangulated Analysis is the Environmental Scan. Because one of the two beginnings of work engagement is motivation, some things we know about motivation also hold true for work engagement. Herzberg (1959) argued that the things that contributed to motivation were not the same as the things that prevented motivation. These factors in the environment effect engagement in a similar way. If they are strong enough, they drain away existing engagement and make it difficult, if not impossible, to build any momentum toward increasing engagement.

Brody worked in a filthy office. Trash was rarely

emptied and the carpet hadn't seen a vacuum in months. Brody was disgusted by the filth and felt that the condition of the workplace reflected how little the owners of the business cared about him or his colleagues. As recognition for his department's meeting a tough deadline, Pete, one of the owners, sent them an email congratulating them and gave them all a pen with the company's logo on it. Instead of feeling appreciated, the email and pen just made Brody angry.

Any effort Brody's organization made to increase his motivation would be a wasted effort. The unpleasant working environment was allowing engagement to leak away. Filling a container with a leak can only be temporary. It's only a matter of time before it all leaks out the side. The issue of the substandard working condition was coloring Brody's attitude to everything else in his work environment. Until the work environment is addressed, anything the organization does to motivate Brody is going to be perceived as insincere. Improving Brody's work environment wouldn't suddenly motivate him but it would plug the leak. Once the leak is mended, Brody might respond differently to praise, awards, or gifts.

The power of work engagement is that it generates energy. Factors that interfere with work engagement are referred to as *power drains* because they drain away the energy of engagement. Any major drain that exists must be dealt with if efforts to increase work engagement are going to achieve sustained results.

The ten most common Power Drains are:

- Issues with one or more **co-workers**.
- Issues with the immediate **supervisor**.
- Issues of **fairness** at work.
- Concerns about future **job security** as a result downsizing or re-organizations.
- Concerns about access to **information about change.**
- Aspects or **tasks of the job** that are not enjoyed.
- Necessary **resources** for the job not consistently available.
- **Group dynamics** as a result of members of the work group not "fitting" in.
- Physically unpleasant **work space**.
- **Work volume** too high.

While a good environmental scan will include an evaluation of these ten most common power drains, simply measuring the presence and strength of these power drains is not enough. People can be tremendously resourceful. If asked, they may readily identify the issues they find draining. If you don't go further with your investigation you may not discover they have also put some very effective strategies in place for dealing with these drains.

When people in the environment are coping with a drain, it reduces the degree to which engagement is being affected. These coping strategies reflect resilience in the system and when resilience is present, deal-

Measuring the presence and strength of a power drain is not enough; measuring resilience in the system is also necessary.

ing with a drain can safely be postponed. This will permit you to prioritize your efforts and address those drains that may not be as strong as others but do not have any resilience. These drains are having a bigger negative affect on engagement and work on these will result in a bigger positive change. A good environmental scan will therefore include a method for assessing the resilience in the system as well as measuring the presence and strength of a power drain. Chapter 4 describes the types of power drains in more detail and provides several strategies for measuring them. The alternative to these strategies is to use the Momentum Busines Group's Power Drain Assessment Tool (PDAT). More information regarding this tool is available in Appendix II.

Valued Behavior Assessment (VBA)

The third tool used for diagnostics in the Triangulated Analysis is an assessment process for identifying behaviors most valued and reinforced by the group. A description of the steps to this procedure are available on pages 48 and 49.

The purpose of the Valued Behavior Assessment (VBA) is to identify those behaviors that members of a group reward and punish. Whenever a group of people come together for any length of time a set of unwritten rules and expectations emerge. These rules and expectations make the functioning of the group more effective. They define what behavior is acceptable and unacceptable. Members of the group comply and enforce these rules and expectations. New members are taught them through social rewards and punishments. Members of the group who do not honor them are at first gently punished with sarcastic comments, mild teasing or veiled reprimands. If this

The VBA identifies what behaviors a work group rewards and punishes.

is not sufficient to correct the offending group member, more severe, overt methods are taken that will ultimately result in outright ostracism. Members of a work group who cannot or will not comply with the group's unwritten rules and expectations for behavior will eventually, quit, transfer or get fired.

These rules and expectations are very strong and they dictate what behavior is encouraged and what will be censored. The rules and expectations can work for the organization's goals or against them. In fact, the same expectation can be either, depending on how it is expressed.

Roger's work group provided residential services to six men with developmental disabilities. When the VBA was completed, the strongest behavioral expectation identified was that of ensuring the men they supported had control over choice-making. Since the organization's mission was to "promote meaningful lives" it would seem that this group's expectation was perfectly aligned with the organization's goals. However, in practice choices were honored even when they violated the organization's funding source's regulations. This created a serious problem. The group's behavioral expectation that members would always honor the choices made by the men they were supporting was putting the whole organization's funding in jeopardy! The expectation itself was a good and caring one, but the degree to which it was being implemented made it highly problematic for the organization.

From a work engagement perspective, Roger's group provides a major challenge. These unwritten rules and expectations have persisted over many years because they solved a group problem. In the case of Roger's group, the men they supported could easily become violent. Over the years, members of the work group learned that if they encouraged

When valued behaviors of a work group are understood, conflict with the group's valued behaviors can be avoided. The behaviors valued by the group can then be used to help the group meet organizational goals.

and honored choices of these men, the frequency of violence was dramatically reduced. But now, if the organization dictates that the work group adjust this long-standing expectation that the members of the work group always honors choice, the work group will find themselves between a rock and a hard place. Compliance with the organization's dictates will erode the relationship between group members and will also make their workplace more dangerous. The conflict caused by these two consequences of compliance will significantly reduce their overall engagement.

If, instead, group members comply with the group in defiance of the organization, this creates some tension between them and the organization. Trust and feelings of connectedness to the organization will erode and their sense that the organization valued their work will be damaged. This situation appears to be a no-win, but it doesn't have to be. Instead of creating conflict with the group, the organization can explore a compromise.

Finding ways to honor choices while still complying with the external regulations will take creative problem-solving. But doing so will also serve to enhance work engagement and reduce the probability of lost funding. Before either can be accomplished, the organization needs to take steps to become aware of the values that are important to the work group. Without this information, the opportunity for creating a win-win-win for the group, the customer and the organization is lost.

One More Tool:
The Vision Exam

The Vision Exam is a useful tool for understanding how infused the organization's mission, vision and values are throughout the organization. It is an optional tool and can be used to supplement the VBA as a diagnostic tool for the organization strategy/cultural level. Like the VBA, the Vision Exam is not an instrument but rather a brief set of short answer questions. The Vision Exam appears on page 50.

The Vision Exam can be delivered in a variety of ways. The most common method of delivery is through an email survey, preferably using a third-party software to ensure anonymity. Another way is to use the questions in an interview format or through focus groups. Both of these latter formats

will permit you to probe answers for better understanding but are time intensive (interviewers time,
interviewees time and analysis of qualitative data),
making them expensive options.

A third, rather innovative strategy is to embed the
Vision Exam into software that is being used for es-
tablishing or updating each employee's individualized development plan. When the Vision Exam is
administered this way, it becomes part of the annual
evaluation process. The employee and his or her supervisor are reminded of the strategic direction of
the organization. This increased awareness can be
woven into each person's annual development action plan.

Using the Tools in a Triangulated Analysis

A comprehensive accurate assessment will involve
using all three tools, an engagement assessment, an
environmental scan and a Valued Behavior Assessment (VBA). Individually each tool provides valuable information that can guide action. When used
together, each tool provides shadings and deeper
understanding of the information produced by the
other tools. Triangulated Analysis provides a focused, precise look at the underlying dynamics of a
work environment.

For an even more precise analysis you can use tools
specifically designed for use in a Triangulated Analysis which, when used together comprise the Momentum Triangulated Analysis (MTA) system. The first

element of the MTA is the Work Engagement Assessment Tool (WEAT) which measures the first angle of the analysis. The second MTA tool is the Power Drain Assessment Tool (PDAT) which provides the second angle. More information regarding these tools is available in Appendices I and II. The third angle of the MTA is the Valued Behavior Analysis (VBA) instructions for which are described on pages 48 and 49. The third angle can also optionally include the Vision Exam described on page 50.

The Momentum Triangualted Analysis (MTA) system provides detailed engagement diagnostics that go well beyond traditional information about organizational culture, workplace conditions and employee attitudes. These tools are like an MRI or CAT scan for your organization. With these tools you can avoid subjecting your organization to the risk and disruption of change initiatives that are not precisely fitted to the needs of the organization.

The *Momentum Triangulated Analysis (MTA):*

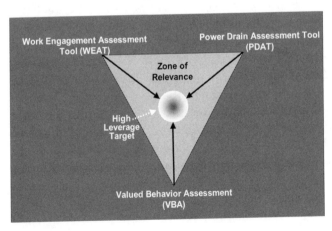

Mike's organization used the Momentum Triangulated Analysis to help his work group. When the WEAT was implemented with his group, the overall score was well above the population norms and scored in the low end of the Usually Engaged zone (More information regarding each of these engagement zones is provided in Appendix I). Mike and his group were pleased with this score but not really surprised because they were known to be a highly effective and innovative group.

Scores on each of the six indicators were, like the total score, all above the population norm. The Relationship and Growth/Challenge indicators, however, were only slightly above and lagged behind the other indicators (See pages 32 and 33 to review the definitions of each of these indicators). That was curious because Mike thought the group cared very much for each other and he believed the organization had provided plenty of opportunities for professional development.

Taken alone, the WEAT scores would suggest that all was well. Mike decided that he wanted a complete picture so the other two tools of the MTA were also implemented. Data from the PDAT indicated that issues with co-workers scored in the Brown-Out zone but when resilience was factored, it was reduced to the Flicker zone (An explanation of each of these zones is available in Appendix II). That indicated that conflict was occurring but not causing serious damage and overall, his folks were managing the conflict.

What Mike was not happy with was the Fairness and Work Volume score. Fairness was in the Brown-

Out zone and Work Volume in the Black-Out zone. In both cases, the data indicated that there was no resilience in the system for dealing with them. This data indicated that his folks were feeling helpless to control either power drain. Mike knew enough about psychology to know that feeling helpless about something could be nothing but bad. He knew that work load had increased for everyone but he was surprised at how much it was weighing on his folks. That might explain the low score on Growth/Challenge. If folks were feeling overwhelmed by their work, it might be hard to take time away to participate in professional development opportunities.

Triangulated Analysis provides a focused, precise look at the underlying dynamics of a work enviornment.

The fairness issue was curious. A sense of fairness is based on many things. Two primary sources of fairness would be fair pay for effort and an equal distribution of work. Since the average income of Mike's group was slightly above the industry average, he didn't think money was the issue. This made him wonder whether work distribution was the issue.

Data from the VBA helped to bring the rest of the data into focus. The two most valued behaviors of his group were excellence and teamwork. Both made sense to Mike. His staff set high standards for themselves. They also expected that everyone would pitch in to achieve those standards. If one member had a problem or a looming deadline, other members were expected to help. Combining the findings of the WEAT with the PDAT information and the VBA, Mike understood what was happening. Work volume was the primary and overwhelming issue and the group expectation for excellence was being enforced despite the increase in volume of work. In addition, the expectation for support from fellow team members was also present. Group members were simultaneously feeling pressured by others to help even though their own work load was consuming. They were also feeling let down when other members were half-heartedly or not pitching in to help them. The result was an erosion of excellence and a growing frustration. This would explain both the fairness and the co-worker score on the PDAT and the relationship score on the WEAT. Mike could see that although the overall WEAT score was currently good, without some action it was unlikely to remain strong over time.

Using a triangulated approach to assessment, the target for effective, and efficient change becomes clearer. In Mike's case, teambuilding in response to the lower relationship indicator on the WEAT may or may not have helped. Its effectiveness would have depended on whether the issues of frustration with the lack of collegial support surfaced during the teambuilding exercises. Without the Triangulated Analysis identifying it as an important issue, there would be no deliberate mechanism for surfacing these issues. It is quite likely the issues would not surface on their own and so they would not be dealt with. By the same token, simply encouraging his folks through reminders to take advantage of professional development opportunities would probably have increased frustration in his staff.

Examining the PDAT in isolation, Mike may have overlooked the implications of the co-worker score, dismissing it because it was in the Flicker zone. He would not have had any way to interpret the fairness score and would not have understood the role expectations for excellence was playing in magnifying the effect of an increased work load.

Finally, without the data from the WEAT and the PDAT, Mike may have interpreted the valued behaviors of excellence and teamwork to be all positive. In fact, these expected behaviors were playing a significant role in jeopardizing future work engagement.

Using the MTA to triangulate the data and create a detailed organizational diagnostic "image" offers a group leader a unique opportunity to make changes that take advantage of strengths, build work engagement and address power drains with effective, efficient action. When dealing with groups of people, one size rarely fits all. Rather than force fitting a strategy for improving work engagement, the triangulated approach allows you to tailor the strategy to exactly the needs and circumstances of the group with which you are working.

The medical metaphor, "at least do no harm" comes to mind. If you can't make it better, at least don't make it worse. The targeted intervention strategies made possible by the level of accuracy provided by triangualation will get the results you want while minimizing resistance.

"No one dies from working too hard.
But when people don't get any recognition in their work,
the stress of that lack of control can kill them."
Barrie S. Greiff

Instructions for Implementing the Valued Behavior Assessment (VBA)

1. Give each member of your work group, including yourself, 10 post-it notes. Ask each member to choose the best 10 words or short 2-3 word phrase to describe the group, writing one on each note.

2. When the group has completed the post-it notes have them place them on a wall in a random manner so that everyone's notes get mixed together.

3. The group will then sort the notes on the wall by moving positive words to the left side of the wall, negative words to the right and neutral or unknown words in the middle.

4. The facilitator helps the group to sort the middle notes into positive or negative by asking the writer what he/she meant by the note.

5. **In silence**, the group now sorts the positive adjectives into themes (e.g. "fun" and "time goes quickly.") As words get moved around, words may be moved to several different clusters. Members keep moving notes until all the notes appear to be in the right clusters. The facilitator will know this when it has been a few minutes since anyone in the group has moved a note.

6. The facilitator helps the group to name the various clusters of notes based on a common theme or underlying concept that captures the core of all the words. Names for clusters need to be a description of a behavior or an attitude.

Names for clusters represent the underlying valued behavior of the group.

7. Negative words represent a protest about something that is lacking and desired by the group. The facilitator helps the group to identify what each negative adjective is protesting and, when possible, places it with a positive group. For example, "rude" might be placed with the cluster "relationships." In some cases, the protest may represent a valued behavior that was not captured in the positive adjectives. For example, several negative adjectives referring to "too many rules" and "bossy" may suggest a value of "freedom." If there are a lot of negative post-it notes it might be wise to sort them into groups using the same procedure used for the positive adjectives. The difference comes in naming the group. Look for what it is that the group is complaining is not present or occurring frequently enough.

Vision Exam

The purpose of this survey is to gauge how well people understand the strategic direction of the organization.

This survey is anonymous and is intended to assess the organization, not you as an individual.

Answer each question as well as you can. It isn't necessary to recite the official wording in response to any of the following questions. Feel free to use your own words. If you do not know the answer to the question, simply write, "Don't know."

1. What is the organization's vision?

2. What is the organization's mission?

3. List the organization's guiding principles or values.

4. How does the work that you do contribute to the organization's ability to achieve its mission?

5. Have you observed examples of actions or decisions the organization has taken that are aligned with its principles or values. Please describe.

6. Have you observed examples of actions or decisions the organization has taken that are not aligned with its principles or values. Please describe.

7. How does the organization's vision, principles or values help you to live out your own personal values?

Chapter 4

Power Drains

"...a stitch in time is worth nine"
Unknown

Work Engagement is a powerful source of energy that provides benefit to both the employee and the employer. There are three approaches available to support and nurture work engagement. The first of these approaches is to deal with those factors in the environment that get in the way of work engagement. These conditions or factors drain energy. You can't fill a sink until you plug the drain and it's the same for work engagement. You cannot increase work engagement until you take care of the leaks and if the leak is large enough, the power of your work engagement is going to drain away. That's why these environmental factors are referred to as Power Drains.

Power drains are irritating, distracting or frustrating. Examples of power drains are a very cold office in the winter, unpleasant music coming from the next cubicle, or rumors about downsizing. It doesn't matter whether the drain is a slow drip, a steady flow or a gushing stream, it wears away at your concentration and your interest and enjoyment in the work. Many power drains start at the minor, slow drip level but, if not dealt with, they can get stronger, until they are overwhelming. When a power drain reaches the gushing level, people experience "burn out." They are "fried" by the energy ebbing away. The result is a toxic environment. Pay now or pay later, power drains cannot be ignored.

For the last three years, Hilary loved her job. She was doing work that she knew she was good at and enjoyed doing. Then, Braydon was hired and things changed. Braydon loved to "chat" and quickly got on a first name basis with everyone in the building. He dominated every meeting and didn't mind "borrowing" other people's ideas and presenting them as his own. He irritated Hilary but she enjoyed her work so she just focused on that. When things got really busy and a critical deadline loomed, Hilary found herself doing a lot of what should have been Braydon's work. Hilary resented it but she did it anyway because she didn't want to let the company or the customers down.

Power Drains can start as a slow drip but, if left unattended, can get stronger, until they are overwhelming.

She complained to her supervisor but his only response was, "Folks upstairs really like Braydon." When a promotional opportunity came up, Hilary applied. When it was announced that Braydon had been awarded the position, she became disheartened. Lately, Hilary is simply doing what she has to and she is actively looking for a better opportunity elsewhere.

Hilary had been a star performer. She was energetic, bright, conscientious, had a positive attitude and she was committed to her career. The slip from engaged to seriously unengaged is a major loss.

Organizations cannot afford to squander such a scarce resource as a highly engaged employee. Hilary's loss of engagement cannot be re-built as long as a power drain is unaddressed. Any progress made on improving Hilary's work engagement will leak away. The focus has to begin with correcting those conditions that are draining her engagement away. Once drains have been corrected, however, some work will then be needed to re-build her engagement.

Types of Power Drains

So what are these power drains? A power drain is anything that is occurring in the work environment that threatens a person's sense of value, purpose, comfort or safety. Safety refers to all aspects of well-being: emotional, physical or financial.

Power drains can come individually or in creative combinations. Just about any time someone says they are feeling "burned out" or "fed up" with their work, you can trace the source to one or more of the power drains.

The ten most common power drains are:

Resource Scarcity:

Needed supplies, equipment, technology, information, labor, or material are not available to you to do your work. Despite their absence, expecta-

Power Drain:
Anything that is occurring in the work environment that threatens a person's sense of value, purpose, comfort or safety.

tions for the quality or quantity of work have not been adjusted. Jill works in a satellite office. When her printer cartridge runs out the main office sends a replacement. Jill's office is not allowed to keep a back up cartridge so Jill can't print until the new cartridge arrives. The demand to continue to produce without adequate resources creates frustration, a sense of helplessness and anger with the organization.

Difficult Co-Worker:

There are many reasons a co-worker can serve as a power drain. Co-workers that don't do their share of the work, have irritating habits, different values, are incompetent or take a lot of sick time that isn't really sick time are just a few examples. It is rare situation in which you are able to choose your co-workers but you spend forty hours a week in frequent, if not continuous, contact with them. It shouldn't be surprising that your relationship with some of these folks may not be great. In a competitive or tense situation, a "not great" relationship can quickly become a very unpleasant, adversarial relationship. Working with people you don't like or don't respect creates a hostile, uncooperative and unhealthy environment.

Unpleasant Physical Work Space:
Temperature, noise, proximity to others, availability and type of light, comfort and utility of the furniture, and cleanliness of the work area all contribute to productivity and morale. Too hot or too cold, too noisy or too quiet: different people need different work environments. For example, research indicates that younger workers raised with video games and the Internet, look for and produce best in noisy environments. This is the opposite condition that works well for their parents. The younger worker often prefers a busy, multi-tasking, stimulating environment. The older worker will be more comfortable in a quiet office. "One size" certainly does not "fit all."

Other physical environment issues include the degree of physical danger in the environment, the risks for long-term health problems, air-quality, access to windows, presence of toxins (mold) or pests (mice, cockroaches), space allocations, etc. It is very difficult to feel good about the organization or the work you do when you are physically uncomfortable or feel that you are physically at risk of injury.

Difficult Boss:
Supervisory positions are not always filled by the right person. Supervision requires a different skill set than a technical position. Despite that, many good technicians are promoted to supervisory positions. When this happens they may flounder if they do not have the skills needed for the new role.

Sometimes the issue is really that your supervisor's style is not a good match for your working style. If, for example, you are most comfortable with a lot of direction and you have a supervisor that expects you to be a self-starter, then there is going to be trouble. Your supervisor is a key gatekeeper to many rewards such as interesting assignments, promotions, or career development opportunities. Lack of confidence in your supervisor or a mismatch in expectations or working styles may leave you feeling trapped and/or vulnerable.

Work Tasks:

The very nature of the work may be a power drain. For some people, repetitive, non-challenging work can result in boredom. If you dislike the actual tasks that are part of the job it is going to take great energy to do the work. You may find yourself in a situation like this when you accept a position because you "need a job." It can also occur when you accept a promotion that does not make use of the skills you most enjoy using or when there is a redesign and your job changes significantly.

Access to Information about Change:

It can be exhausting to work in a situation in which it feels like expectations are a moving target. When you can't get clear direction or if the goals keep changing, frustration builds.

Change is occurring at an unprecedented rate and, with change, fear of the unknown is rampant. In the absence of facts, people tend to fill in the gaps with the worst possible outcomes. It is difficult to keep going when fear takes hold.

Creative problem-solving is an early victim to a culture of fear. The result of constant change is confusion and sometimes, outright chaos regarding shifting roles, priorities and re-designed procedures.

Some people thrive on ambiguity and change, but many more find it extremely upsetting. Depending on the environment you prefer and the level of ambiguity in the environment, this power drain may be a big problem for you or your staff in today's fast changing environment.

Fairness:

When you take a job, you enter into a social contract with your employer. You expect to give your employer a certain level of effort and, in return, you expect your employer will give you certain rewards. If the balance between give and take shifts, there is a loss of respect and trust and the relationship breaks down. Cutbacks in staff result in heavier work loads for those who remain but staff are rarely compensated for the extra work they are expected to do.

Being passed over for promotion in favor of someone who you do not believe is as qualified, watching a co-worker abuse his or her sick time with no consequences or feeling like your work load is heavier than your co-workers can upset the precarious balance. When the balance between what you give and what you get shifts so that it feels like you're giving more than you are getting, anger and resentment can take hold.

Group Dynamic:

A set of individuals may each get along with the others but when you put them together as a group, friction, competition, and poor co-operation sometimes surface. This dysfunction is usually based on unresolved issues that can be ignored when dealing one-on-one. But in a group setting, the complication of multiple simultaneous interactions magnifies the interpersonal issues between group members.

Dysfunctional behavior can range from passive obstruction or contrariness to open hostility and aggression. Regardless, the dysfunction makes it difficult, if not impossible, for the group to get anything done. What does get done is either not done well or is undone or re-done by a group member later. Tension is high and members resort to avoiding the group or going around the group to get things done.

Another issue associated with work groups is the culture that develops. When two or more people work together for any length of time, a set of behavioral norms and group values form. These norms and values form the basis of an informal set of rules or code. This code is important because it clarifies expectations and helps the group function. They provide some guidance about the appropriate or most effective behavior in a range of situations. The rules or code also provide a sense of predictability and stability because members know what other members of the group are likely to do. When new members join the group, they are pressured to conform to this code. The reward for doing so is acceptance and support. The punishment for not conforming is the group ignores them and sometimes deliberately takes action that will harm the new member's reputation, property or safety. The poor fit of one member causes distress for all because the lack of conformity challenges the code and threatens the stability the code provides.

Work Volume:

A common power drain is the sheer volume of work. When there is more work than can reasonably be completed in the time allotted to it, you have to work a lot harder, a lot smarter, or be a lot less fussy about quality. Any of the alternatives are stressful. One element of this power drain can be centered around the stress and sense of inadequacy created when quality is compromised for work load quantity. A too heavy workload can result from an unanticipated growth in demand, downsizing, or poor estimating. One unfortunate way work load can grow can be a direct result of being reliable. When a supervisor has a high profile or high stakes project, he or she will naturally want to assign it to his or her star performer. Over time, this star performer is taking on more than his or her share of the work. This is an insidious habit and when it emerges, consistently producing a high quality of work can put this worker at risk of burn out.

Lack of Job Security:

It once was true that if you took a job with a large company, you could expect that if you worked hard and followed the rules, you would have a job for life. Those days are gone. Despite the data demonstrating the consistently poor bottom-line results of attempting to improve profitability through downsizing, companies still do it. Several waves of lay-offs creates a climate of fear. The mere whisper of an impending layoff can spark a wildfire of speculation. Concentration, creativity and clear thinking shrink, and trust and loyalty for the organization disappear.

Consequences of Power Drains

All ten of these power drains represent conditions in the environment that you, as one member of the organization, cannot directly control. Despite your lack of control they do affect your ability to do your work. In their early stages they are an irritant, a distraction, or a small puddle in your way. They rarely go away on their own and more commonly they develop into much bigger issues. Hilary's situation with her co-worker Braydon is an example of how a drain can develop. Without attention, drains can become crippling.

Ten Power Drains
- Resource Scarcity
- Difficult Co-Worker
- Unpleasant Work Space
- Difficult Boss
- Work Tasks
- Access to Information about Change
- Fairness
- Group Dynamics
- Work Volume
- Lack of Job Security

Power drains become crippling because, over time, they create the phenomenon of "learned helplessness." Martin Seligman (1975) first identified this phenomenon in his research on stress. Seligman demonstrated that if you subjected animals to a stressor (a mild painful stimulation), the animal would seek out an escape. If none of the strategies for escape were successful, over successive trials the animal would resign itself to enduring the discomfort and not bother trying to find an escape. When, in later trials, Seligman created an obvious escape route, such as an open door, the animal would do nothing to help itself. Instead of exiting through the open door, it would just lie down as it had always done in the past and endure the discomfort. These animals developed ulcers and other stress related illnesses. The animal had learned that efforts to escape would not be successful so even when escape was possible, the animal did not try.

The fact that Hilary was looking for a new opportunity suggests that she had not yet reached Seligman's learned helplessness state. She had, however, reached a point where she no longer felt it worth her while to put in her full effort on the job. If repeated efforts at finding an alternative are not successful, then a sense of being trapped will creep in, along with its partner, learned helplessness. With learned helplessness comes a slide from engaged to unengaged and, if allowed to continue, an even further slide into full disengagement. Hilary is headed for that slippery slope.

You don't have direct control over a power drain so you cannot turn it off. If you have made efforts to change conditions and have been consistently ineffective, you are at risk of giving up in a similar manner *"Learned Helplessness" occurs when repeated efforts to escape an unpleasant stimulus are not successful.*

as the animals in Seligman's experiment did. This is how learned helplessness can creep into a work environment. Apathy, cynicism and depression emerge. Like the animals in the experiment, a side-effect for employees who have given up trying to make a difficult situation better is a host of physical consequences. Being subjected to unpleasant conditions with no control is a highly stressful situation. Both productivity and morale are damaged. This is a prescription for seriously disengaged employees.

When you do not have control over a power drain, you cannot turn it off. This puts you at serious risk of slipping into a learned helpless state.

Diagnosing Power Drains

Before discussing the actions that can be taken to deal with the various power drains, you need to be able to identify which power drains in your work environment are in most need of attention. Assessment is the key to taking steps to stem the loss of power and to addressing the most urgent drain.

Several strategies for diagnosing the type and strength of a power drain are available. Using any combination of the following tools will give you a pretty accurate picture of both the urgency and the appropriate targets for work.

The diagnosis tools are:
1. Observational Assessment
2. Facilitated Assessment by Work Group

3. Instrumented Assessment: Power Drain Assessment Tool (PDAT)

Assessment Method #1: Observation Assessment of Power Drains

This is the simplest and most obvious strategy. Since you are now aware of the top ten power drains, you can begin looking around for them. How many power drains are present in your work environment? How serious are your power drains?

A first step in your observation process would be to examine existing data for suggestions of problems. Primary indicators of serious power drains are:

- Absenteeism
- Turnover
- Chronic and pervasive tardiness
- Work injuries
- Theft
- Vandalism
- Non-compliance with key organizational policies and procedures.

Each of these listed behaviors frequently indicate a power drain is present because they are each sourced in the perception that the organization doesn't care about them or can't be trusted. If you don't feel like you matter or anyone appreciates the work you do, it is hard to come to work each day. A small ache or pain is excuse enough to stay home. Eventually, people quit and leave. Some people quit and don't leave and that is even worse because they are holding a spot that could otherwise be productive. Tardiness, theft, vandalism and ignoring the rules are all based on a sense that the organization is taking more than it is giving. The employee is simply taking back, unofficially, what he or she feels is owed to him or her. The issue of injuries is a little different. Injuries occur more frequently when people are stressed. When power drains are present, people are likely to be feeling stress and less attentive to details. The result is they are more likely to suffer an accident.

For each of these indicators, there may be explanations other than a power drain. But, when these indicators are high or more than one is higher than usual, you may want to question whether power drains are a factor.

If you suspect the presence of power drains, the next step would be to identify which power drains exist and how urgent each is. Each power drain has its own indicators you can look for.

Observational Indicators of Power Drains

Co-Worker
- Inter-personal tensions that carry over from one week to the next
- Complaints about co-workers
- Co-operation between co-workers is poor
- Hesitancy or objection to working with a specific co-worker
- Social pattern for lunch or breaks has changed

Work Volume
- Staff consistently working more than 40 hours
- Increase in errors due to inattention
- Important-but-not-urgent tasks are not done
- More impatience between co-workers
- Overall quality of work has slipped

Work Tasks
- Increase in complaints about the job
- Productivity has decreased
- Increase in socializing between certain employees
- More off-task behavior (computer games, newspaper etc.)
- More personal business being conducted

Group Dynamics
- One employee has more interpersonal problems with the work group
- Difficult behaviors of one staff who leaves re-emerges in a different staff
- Poor attendance or late arrivals at group meetings
- Poor participation and lots of side activity during group meetings
- High negative emotions during group meetings
- Sarcasm and frequent teasing between group members
- Certain procedures or practices exist that you cannot seem to eliminate
- New members' attitudes change within a couple of weeks of starting
- New members to the group have quit or requested a transfer

Scarce Resources
- The budget for certain needed resources has been cut
- Staff are hoarding a particular resource
- Frequent complaints that a resource is not available
- Tensions between staff over access to a resource
- Lack of resources blamed when goals are not met

Physical Work Space
- Complaints about an aspect of the physical environment
- Increase in work injuries or illness directly related to work conditions
- Specific behaviors in response to a physical environment issue (shorts in winter, heavy coats in summer)
- Tensions between staff regarding an environmental issue (room temperature, lighting, level of noise, etc.)
- Requests for purchase of equipment to compensate for an environmental issue (fans, space heaters, earplugs, etc.)

Job Security
- Experienced a lay-off in past 12 months
- Questions about potential lay-offs
- Downturn in organization's revenue in last 12 months
- Competitors have recently laid people off
- Other organizations in geographic area have laid people off

Access to Information about Change
- Recent large-scale re-organization
- Change in senior management
- Industry is changing quickly
- Many policy or procedural changes recently

Fairness
- HR decisions are challenged
- Grievances being filed with the union or a union is being formed
- Requests for clarification of HR policies
- Decrease in cooperation between co-workers
- Complaints about unfair treatment

Difficult Boss (You)

The perception of a difficult boss can be the result of several factors, some of which you may have little control over. Perceptions do not have to be based on reality to influence behavior or to affect the interpretation of other people's behavior. It is important to avoid defensiveness and honestly gauge your employees perceptions if you want to be able to change them.

- Conversation stops abruptly or clearly changes when you enter the room.
- Your employees are going to your supervisor with concerns or for information and help
- Your supervisor is coming to you with complaints from your staff
- Your employees are appealing to other external authority to intervene (HR, legal, union, etc.)
- Staff are withholding or delaying giving you important information

Difficult Boss (Your Supervisor)

Your supervisor may be the source of the problem. Actions by your supervisor cascade down, affecting your employee's ability to work. When this is the case, you won't need a set of questions to detect it because you are as much affected as your employees.

Assessment Method #2:
Facilitated Assessment of Power Drains

This method uses a focus group format. A group of 6-12 employees gather with a facilitator to discuss their perceptions of the power drains. It is the least effective of the assessment strategies because it asks employees to focus on problems and to do so in a group setting. In such a setting, one person's perceptions can influence other participants' perceptions.

In addition, this focus on the negative can create a "self-fulfilling prophecy." Having been sensitized to problems, employees are now noticing issues that previously had not been perceived as a problem but now become evidence of the issues discussed during the group meeting. One other issue that can occur is that the source of a power drain could be a participant in the focus group. In this case, the group may become confrontational or very quiet.

Despite these drawbacks, Facilitated Assessments also have some advantages. Conducting such a meeting delivers a message that employee's input is important. The format permits the gathering of a lot of data quickly and synergy of ideas between the participants.

Conducting a Facilitated Assessment by Work Groups:

- Develop a set of questions in advance of the meeting;
- Allow flexibility in the order of questions but be sure all questions are asked of every group;
- Use a neutral and objective facilitator;
- Have one or two people who are not participants record the comments on flip chart paper so all participants can see what is being noted;
- Ensure that all participants in a group are at the same level in the organization (i.e., don't mix supervisors and line-staff);
- Explain the process that will be used to ensure that people are safe to say what they want to say in the room.

Conducting focus groups can produce rich information if they are skillfully conducted. If not, the information can be misleading. Participants must believe that they are safe from recriminations or they won't tell the truth. You may be tempted to facilitate the focus group yourself. If so, resist the temptation. The quality and reliability of information will be much better if you use a facilitator the participants perceive as neutral and therefore safe.

Assessment Method #3: Instrumented Assessment of Power Drains:

The best method to fully diagnose power drains is to use an instrumented assessment tool. There are a variety of tools that can be used, some of which are more effective than others. A search of the Internet will produce some free tools that can be adapted to give you information about power drains. Other tools can be purchased through publishers of organizational development or performance improvement books. While tools obtained this way can be useful, they were not designed to specifically measure power drains and will therefore require some adaptation and interpretation on your part.

Another option is to develop your own assessment tool. If you are confident in your skill in writing objective, targeted survey questions, then this is quite reasonable. The issue with this option is that it is difficult to write survey questions well. People may interpret your words differently than you intended. If this happens, you will be at risk of misinterpreting the information you gather.

As discussed in Chapter 3, the best way to assess power drains in the work environment is by using the Momentum Business Group's Power Drain Assessment Tool (PDAT). More information regarding the PDAT is available in Appendix II.

AMP's: Reducing Power Loss Due to Power Drains

Once you have determined your most urgent power drains, you now know where to focus energy to minimize the drain. AMP's describe three levels of action that can be taken to minimize a power drain:

A = *Adjust: Change your behavior.*
This is the simplest, least intrusive level of action and should, in most cases, be used first. While this is the simplest action to take, it is also the least stable. Behaviors will quickly re-emerge if follow-up and follow-through is not maintained.

M = *Move: Change environment.*
This second level of action is more dramatic, in that it will involve changing familiar surroundings. It also has the potential for more enduring results. It is more intrusive than Adjust actions and is therefore resisted more strongly.

P = *Part Company: Leave or be asked to leave.*
This is obviously the most permanent change. It should only be used when other strategies have

not achieved the desired results. There is a high risk of negative repercussions (law suits, demoralization of remaining staff, etc.) so it should be approached with caution and care. It should always be viewed as a default action.

Actions to address Power Drains:
Adjust or Move

For each of the power drains, there are different strategies that can be applied for the Adjust and Move levels. A matrix identifying the appropriate Adjust and Move strategies for each power drain is provided in Appendix III.

Returning to Hilary's situation, she was exposed to three power drains: difficult co-worker, a difficult supervisor and a sense of unfairness. It began as a flicker with the difficult co-worker. When Braydon's behavior resulted in Hilary picking up the slack to make sure the department met a critical deadline, the unfairness power drain was added to the original power drain. The combined effect was a brownout. Hilary was feeling taken advantage of and annoyed enough to seek out a resolution.

If things had been satisfactorily resolved at the point of the brown-out when she sought help from her supervisor, Hilary's level of energy would have been quickly re-instated. Her loyalty to the organization may even have been strengthened as a result. Instead, she was confronted with a third power drain, a difficult boss. For political reasons, Hilary's boss was unwilling to support her and more importantly, he was quite willing to allow Hilary to continue to

carry more than her share of the work load, potentially adding still another power drain to the mix
(work volume). This combination of power drains
was fatal to Hilary's sense of *organizational affinity* and
recognition. She could no longer trust that the organization was going to be
fair with her or that the
organization valued her
contribution. Braydon's
"chatting" was appar-
ently more valued than
her actual productivity.

Ordinarily, it is the supervisor who can have the most leverage to address a power drain.

So, what can be done to repair the situation?

Ordinarily, it is a supervisor who has the most leverage to address a power drain but in this case, the supervisor is part of the problem. Addressing the power drains will need to be done by either Hilary or
someone other than her immediate supervisor. Since
Braydon has already been awarded the promotion,
the co-worker power drain has disappeared. The issue of the difficult boss and a perception of unfairness and work load remain. There are many ways to
address these power drains, some of which Hilary
can take on herself, if she chooses. Hilary's loss of
engagement doesn't have to be permanent. Knowing which power drains are in effect, however, is the
key to taking the most effective corrective action.

Choosing which action to use for each circumstance
is an art not a science. Frequently you will need to
use more than one action. Melissa's accounting department was made up of two groups: receivables
who didn't like payables and vice versa. This division caused all kinds of problems for Melissa. With
the help of her HR department, Melissa planned a

one-day retreat and a set of teambuilding exercises to be used in regular team meetings after the retreat. She instituted some cross-training and reorganized the work to break down the functional division. Over a period of three months, both the quality and quantity of work improved. Individually, none of these Adjust moves would have been enough to change the behavior of the two groups but when combined, she got a major shift. The PDAT identified the issues that needed to be addressed and served as a guide when Melissa selected her actions.

Ordinarily, Adjust actions are your best choice with which to begin, but occasionally you may need to start with a Move action. Lori and Holly were like fire and water together. They were both good staff and capable of quality work but having them both in a staff meeting was a challenge. They couldn't agree on anything making it hard to get anything done in the meetings. Megan, their supervisor, didn't think teambuilding was appropriate because the issue seemed to be between the two of them. When a colleague mentioned he needed some help, Megan offered to assign Holly. Holly was a good match for the new assignment and both Holly's and *Choosing which action to use for each circumstance is an art not a science. But data from the PDAT will dramatically improve your potential for precision.* Lori's productivity improved. More importantly to Megan, team meetings were less emotional and other team members seemed relieved by the change. Megan took advantage of an opportunity to use a move to solve her problem and it worked because the move was a win-win. Both Holly and the organization benefited from the change. This is critical to a move solution. If Holly was not well-suited to the new assignment, Megan would simply be dumping a problem and, in the long run, everyone will pay a price as a result of the move.

Actions to address Power Drains:
Parting Company

Using an Adjust or Move action is always prefer-able to this third action, Parting Company. When a power drain has reached the Black-Out level, how-ever, there may be no other choice and it may be the best action for both the organization and the individual. Parting company involves a permanent change. When Victor could not get a team to align itself with the organization's goals, he dissolved the team and reassigned all its members to other depart-ments. This is a drastic but permanent move. Alisha met with Nancy about her high absentee rate and her poor relationship with fellow team members. Nancy admitted she didn't like her job and didn't see any future. They came to the agreement that it was time for Nancy to move on and she turned in her two-week notice that afternoon. Once again, Parting Company involves a permanent change and should not be undertaken lightly.

Permanent changes look simpler than they are and, as a result, they are sometimes used too soon. If not handled well, they can result in legal ramifications and there are often emotional consequences for re-maining staff to deal with. When someone is dis-missed, even someone disliked by most of the staff, feelings of guilt or fear are stirred up. You may find staff suddenly sympathetic to the very person they were previously bad-mouthing.

If you have considered other alternatives and you are convinced that the best action is truly to Part Company then tread carefully! Be as fair and honest with the employee that must leave as possible and put some effort into strengthening trust with those employees who remain. Forewarned is forearmed!

Adjust is usually your best choice to begin with. Occasionaly you may need to start with Move. Parting Company should only be used as a last resort.

Power Restoration

Once you have achieved some movement in the right direction, to properly repair your power drain you have three additional steps that need to follow your Adjust, Move or Part Company strategies. Power Restoration steps will help you to stabilize the new behaviors or environment and gain some long-term permanence. Just fixing the Power Drain will not restore the organization to full health. Like rehabilitation therapy is necessary after a serious injury, Power Restoration provides a focused effort to regain engagement losses caused by the Power Drain(s). To be effective, these steps should be done together.

These essential follow-up steps are:
- Reframe
- Really listen
- Respectfully reinforce

Reframe

A frame is something that surrounds and supports a picture. If you change the frame around a picture, you can dramatically change your perception of the picture. Colors you hadn't noticed before now become pronounced. Features that dominated may now be subdued. What surrounds the picture changes what you notice in the picture. In the same way, if you change the frame around an event, you change how you perceive the event. Someone arriving late to a meeting can be viewed as either uncaring or conscientious, depending on whether you believe the individual didn't care enough to be on time or cared enough to come, even though he had to be late. Same event, two very different perceptions depending on the frame you put around the event.

Once you have plugged a Power Drain, it is time to change the frame that surrounds it. This will allow employees to focus on different aspects of the same picture. Reframing involves three steps. The first step is *validating feelings* by admitting to your employees that prior to the Adust, Move or Part Company action, things were not acceptable. The second step involves providing *evidence that things have now changed*. The third and most important step requires that you get *employees to describe, out loud, what has changed*. By having employees label the change themselves, they are more likely to accept that it really has changed.

Germaine's staff had struggled for a few months with what they described as "a moving target." The organization had a new CEO and priorities seemed to change daily. Germaine worked with his supervisor to get some clarification on organizational directions. He then guided his staff in developing a set of prioritized goals that were in line with his understanding of the new organizational direction. He posted the set of goals on a bulletin board in the lunchroom. When a decision had to be made between priorities, Germaine would refer to the plan to answer questions from staff. After a month, Germaine called a staff meeting to review the plan. He started the meeting by having each person give an example of how the plan had helped make priorities less confusing. He then asked for input on updating or adjusting goals for the next 30 days.

Germaine's third step, getting his staff to describe how the change had helped them, is the most critical of the three steps. It will take the most creativity to implement. Unless employees can describe for themselves how things have changed, they will not believe or accept it and the frame does not change. Things will quickly slip back to the way they were.

Really Listen
The importance and power of listening cannot be underestimated. Listening to someone is a gift to the other person. It creates a connection between the listener and the speaker and builds trust. As a follow-up to Adjust, Move and Part Company actions and either after or while reframing the power drain, listening can have a tremendous impact.

Your employees bring a number of problems, concerns, and complaints to you as their supervisor. When they do, a natural response is to jump in and "fix" things. If you discipline yourself to wait, to ask the right questions, to clarify and paraphrase what you heard, you can lead your staff to solve their own problems. When staff find their own answers, they are far more likely to be committed to implement-

Listening to someone is a gift to the other person. It creates a connection and builds trust.

ing them. In addition, you don't have to waste time selling them on the logic and merits of an answer. As an extra bonus, you have contributed to your employee's sense of mastery, self-esteem and knowledge pool. The next time that employee confronts a similar issue, he or she will be more confident about risking an independent solution.

Jacob flopped into a chair in John's office. "I can't get that blasted machine to run properly." John knew that the machine had been an issue but he also knew that it had been fixed. It would have been easy to remind Jacob that the repairman had been in and others had been quite pleased with the improved performance. Instead, he sat still and asked, "What's the problem?" When Jacob explained, John's impulse was to tell Jacob the problem wasn't with the machine, the problem was with Jacob. Instead he asked, "So, what have you tried?" After a couple more questions Jacob seemed to calm down. He said "There's a couple of things I didn't try, I'll go back." But Jacob didn't get up so John asked, "Is there something else?" "Yeah, I'm feeling really pressured, that copier was just the last straw," "Okay," John said, "What's up?" "I'm just not comfortable with turning in that report." With a little more probing, John was able to help Jacob identify what he could do to improve the quality of the report. The problem had never been the photocopier. When you fix the problem presented, you risk losing the opportunity to help with the real problem, the bigger problem. Listening can be a very good deal for you. The key is to control your impulse to be the "answer-giver."

Respectfully Reinforce

Reinforcing is nothing more than noticing when something positive has occurred and saying so. Rita told Keith "If you don't hear from me, you're doing fine." That is an unfortunate attitude because Rita is hurting herself as much as Keith. Saying something nice to someone builds your own sense of well-being when that person smiles in return. Praise is a classic win-win.

Thorndike's Law of Effects (1932) states that a person will increase a behavior if he or she finds the consequence of that behavior pleasant. That is a pretty straightforward law and by that law, you would predict that if you praised an employee, that employee would increase the frequency of the behavior that was praised. It doesn't work quite that way, does it? The key is the phrase *"finds* the consequence *pleasant."* Adults are complicated. What you find pleasant, someone else might hate. Lance is an intensely shy person. His supervisor praised him publicly at a staff meeting for a report he had written. Lance was red in the face and couldn't sit down fast enough. It is unlikely Lance found that public praise very pleasant. It was more likely experienced as punishing. No wonder managers complain, "I tried that re-

Thorndike's Law of Effects states that responses that are accompanied or followed by satisfaction (i.e., a reward, or what was later to be termed a reinforcement) will be more likely to reoccur, and those which are accompanied by discomfort (i.e., a punishment) will be less likely to reoccur.

inforcing stuff and it didn't work."

Respectfully reinforcing means a manager cannot take a "one size fits all" approach to dealing with his or her staff. He or she must carefully match the reinforcer to the needs and prefer-ences of the em-ployee. This means that the supervisor will need to know

> **Respectfully   Reinforcing** *involves carefully matching the reinforcer to the needs and preferences of the employee.*

a little about each employee.   A private comment to Lance would have been much more effective.

A tool to help supervisors reinforce more effectively is available on pages 85-88. This tool asks an employ-ee to identify the kind of rewards he or she likes and what kinds of things he or she hates. With informa-tion like this Lance's supervisor can avoid punishing Lance when he or she intended to reward him.

Praise is usually the first thing people think of when they hear the term "reinforcer." Praise certainly is a commonly used reinforcer but the only reason it has any affect on behavior is because it is valued. Value is based on the degree of trust or respect you feel for the person delivering the praise. A reinforcers' strength depends on respect and/or trust. Without one or the other, the praise has little or no value.

A possible exception to this comes to mind. The en-tertainer is highly reinforced by praise in the form of clapping. The people clapping are usually strangers to the entertainer. It would appear that trust and re-spect don't enter into this situation. Appearances can be deceiving. An entertainer respects his audience's judgement. When the audience enthusiastically applauds, the performer trusts that this is evidence of the audiences' approval. So, trust and respect are very much a part of this interaction even though it is not immediately obvious.

You earn trust and respect every day. When you give your staff your attention, you make a point to say hello in the morning, or you ask how he or she is feeling upon returning from a work absence, you earn trust and respect. All of these behaviors deliver the same message, "You matter."

Jose had been working on a special project and had just submitted the final report to his supervisor, Erika. After reading the report Erika went to Jose's office to talk about it and get Jose's ideas on how the information in the report could best be used. She didn't actually say the report was good. But, the fact that she went to the trouble of going to Jose's office, she clearly intended to use the report and she wanted Jose's input on how best to do so, communicated a strong message of approval to Jose.

Nick heard at a workshop that his relationship with staff would have a direct impact on their productivity. He had always prided himself on being a multitasker but he decided that when staff came into his office he would stop what he was doing and give them his full attention. The first few times he did so he noticed some surprise from his staff. He also began to notice that he was getting more and better information from them. They seemed more willing to stop by his office and when he asked them to do something extra, there didn't seem to be as much resistance. Such a simple change - but sometimes the most powerful changes are that simple. Taking the time to give his employees his full attention communicated they were important and what they had to say was important.

Jordan's new boss Andrew interrupted her to ask for a special report for a meeting that afternoon. Jordan was working on another project which she reluctantly set aside and got to work on Andrew's report. When she brought the report to Andrew an hour later he said, "Thank you, I really needed this." Jordan was surprised by Andrew's response to the report. After all, it was her job to get that kind of information to her supervisor. She responded with the only thing she could think of, "You're welcome." But as she walked away, she smiled to herself.

It's these little things that add up to the kind of relationship that has reinforcing power. What you say matters but what you DO matters more. What you say will not have the effect you want unless you have built a trusting or respectful relationship. Research indicates

The number one reason people stay or leave a job is their relationship with their supervisor.

that the number one reason people leave a job is a poor relationship with a supervisor. That puts a lot on your shoulders but it also means that you have a lot of power to make the work environment a better place to be.

If reinforcing behavior feels awkward to you don't give up or decide this isn't for you. Rather than focus on reinforcing your employees, your efforts would be better spent on earning their respect and trust every day. It's the little things that will make the difference and if you are working on building such a relationship, the reinforcing will happen naturally.

Supervisors and Power Drains

Power drains drive turnover, contribute to absenteeism, theft, vandalism, conflict and every other factor that affects prodictivity and morale. They rarely go away on their own. More often they grow like a cancer in the organization. Dealing with power drains is a supervisor's job. Many power drains fall within the realm and authority of the supervisor.

Learning to diagnose power drains is a big step to improving the workplace. An even bigger step is learning to successfully apply the various actions to change them. Organizations hire the entire person. What goes on in people's heads and hearts affects what they produce. The supervisor that recognizes this is way ahead. This supervisor understands that dealing with power drains early creates conditions for maximum productivity from his or her staff. It also creates a place where people want to work.

Supervisors have a LOT of influence on the work environment. It is possible for you to make the work environment better for at least your own staff.

You will no sooner get one power drain under control and you will notice another. This is because power drains are a given in any organizational environment. Power drains will vary in intensity so the most urgent power drain will capture your attention. Once it is no longer urgent, your tolerance for another power drain will shift, even if its intensity does not change. Relative to all other power drains, it has become the most urgent. It will help you if you can put power drains into the right perspective.

Some power drains you will be able to deal with one-to-one with the staff member that is affected by it. More often, the power drain will be affecting several of your staff and when that is so, you will use a more general response. Start with the Adjust actions and if necessary, add a Move action. As a last resort, you may need to add the Parting Company action.

Regardless of which action or group of actions you use, follow-up with the three power restoration steps. Helping your staff to reframe their experience and being optimistic about the future will add energy. Really listening will help you to avoid wasting energy on the wrong problems. It will also help you to build increased capacity for dealing with problems within your staff. Finally, respectfully reinforcing builds trust and respect, and increases your influence with your staff. It also helps to heal the bad effects caused by prolonged exposure to a power drain. These three steps will help you ensure that positive changes you have created by dealing with power drains will last.

"The final test of a leader is that he leaves behind him in other men the conviction and the will to carry on."

Walter Lippman

Respectful Recognition
What Works for You?

Directions: *Please review the following list.*

- *Put a check mark beside all of the things you like.*
- *After reviewing the entire list, go back and put a circle around the checkmark of the five things you like the most.*
- *Go through the list one more time and put an X beside the five things you dislike the most.*

____ 1. *Receive positive verbal feedback at a staff meeting.*

____ 2. *Be asked to take on a tough problem or new challenge.*

____ 3. *Be asked to give a presentation on your work at a staff meeting or a company conference.*

____ 4. *Receive positive, handwritten comments in the margin of a document you prepared.*

____ 5. *Invited to a social event at the home of your boss.*

____ 6. *Given the opportunity to work flexible hours or to work at home.*

____ 7. *Given the opportunity to purchase new tools and equipment to enhance your work.*

____ 8. *Have your picture and a story about your work appear in the organization or community newspaper.*

____ 9. *Asked for your opinion on a difficult organizational problem or a new business opportunity.*

____ 10. *Given the opportunity to speak about your work at an important professional conference.*

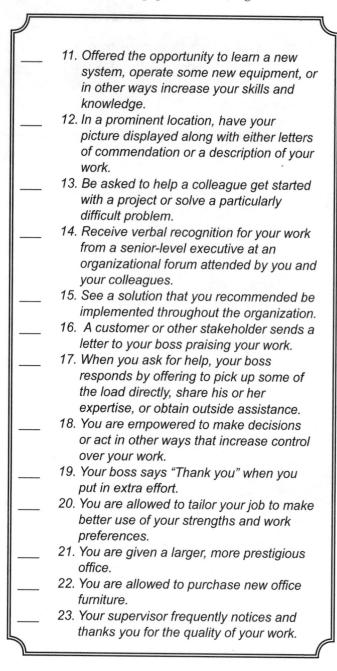

___ 11. Offered the opportunity to learn a new system, operate some new equipment, or in other ways increase your skills and knowledge.

___ 12. In a prominent location, have your picture displayed along with either letters of commendation or a description of your work.

___ 13. Be asked to help a colleague get started with a project or solve a particularly difficult problem.

___ 14. Receive verbal recognition for your work from a senior-level executive at an organizational forum attended by you and your colleagues.

___ 15. See a solution that you recommended be implemented throughout the organization.

___ 16. A customer or other stakeholder sends a letter to your boss praising your work.

___ 17. When you ask for help, your boss responds by offering to pick up some of the load directly, share his or her expertise, or obtain outside assistance.

___ 18. You are empowered to make decisions or act in other ways that increase control over your work.

___ 19. Your boss says "Thank you" when you put in extra effort.

___ 20. You are allowed to tailor your job to make better use of your strengths and work preferences.

___ 21. You are given a larger, more prestigious office.

___ 22. You are allowed to purchase new office furniture.

___ 23. Your supervisor frequently notices and thanks you for the quality of your work.

____ 24. You have the freedom to choose when and how frequently you take breaks.

____ 25. You are given an opportunity to attend training for personal and/or skill development.

____ 26. The whole department/team participates in a social event.

____ 27. Your Supervisor helps you to set goals that will help you develop your career.

____ 28. You are given a certificate, trophy or plaque for an outstanding effort.

____ 29. A senior manager comes to your work area to learn what you do.

____ 30. You attend a coffee-time with the senior manager of the organization you are given an opportunity to share your perspective on issues.

____ 31. Information about the budget is shared with you in an honest and complete manner.

____ 32. You are allowed time to exercise during the day.

____ 33. You are allowed to spend a day in another office or work area to learn about their work.

____ 34. You are given a "prime" parking spot.

____ 35. You are given tuition assistance for a college degree of your choice.

____ 36. You are given a cell phone, Blackberry, or laptop.

____ 37. You attend a conference of choice.

____ 38. You are awarded compensatory time for overtime worked.

____ 39. You are asked to represent your supervisor at a meeting.

____ 40. You receive a personal letter from a senior manager of the organization.

Chapter 5

Power Boosts

"Trust men and they will be true to you; treat them greatly,
and they will show themselves great."
Ralph Waldo Emerson

Turn of the century management practices were opposite to Emerson's perspective. These practices were based on the assumption that the way to ensure productivity was to control and threaten employees. While more effective management models have long been available, this old command-and-control model persists. The reason it continues to hang on is because, in the short-term, punishment and fear do get results. At least in the begininning, threats do get people's attention. But, after awhile, people either get used to the punishment or they learn how to avoid it. In either case, the threats no longer have the same effect.

A side-effect of the command-and-control model, however, is that while it can get short-term results, it also shuts down creativity, risk-taking and initiative. The threat of punishment teaches people that they cannot take a chance. The result is that they limit themselves to actions that are familiar and safe. When problems or challenges emerge that require new and different approaches, a workforce managed through fear and punishment can not respond effectively.

In the long-run, treating employees with respect and as a valued-resource consistently produces outstanding organizational results. A workforce treated as a partner will be engaged which means the organization is getting the benefit of its employees' best thinking and best efforts. That is what Power Boosts are about.

There are three tools to help the organization treat its employees as partners. The three tools are:

- *Vision Alignment,*
- *Valued Behavior Alignment*
- *Action Alignment.*

Vision Alignment is focused on the individual, *Valued Behavior Alignment* deals with work groups and teams, and *Action Alignment* addresses organization-wide strategic/cultural issues. All three tools seek to create a better match between the total organization and the people who make up the organization.

Creating better alignment with the organization is important because, so far, forward momentum created by the Power of Three is

Treating employees as a valued partner will increase engagement and as a result, the organization will benefit from the employee's best thinking and best effort.

being fueled by the efforts and initiative of the individual and supervisors. Antonio has worked hard at improving his work team and he systematically removed two serious Power Drains. Things were working well and the team was getting more done with what seemed like much less effort. Soon after, top-management put an incentive program in place that had the effect of putting his team members in competition with one another. That was exactly the opposite effect Antonio was working toward.

Jade, like Antonio, had also worked on improving the work engagement of her team. To address the co-worker and work volume power drains she had championed cross-training and a mentoring program. These actions fit with the organization's stated value that promoted employee development. When the budget got tight, however, her supervisor halted both the cross-training and mentoring program. Jade's supervisor said they were too expensive and interfered with the real work of the department. Jade knew that it was time for her to start looking for a new job.

In both cases the organization is out of "sync" with its employees. The organization has to be a partner in the co-generation of work engagement or the system is out of balance. A win-win-win can only be achieved if all stakeholders are equally committed.

The top 10 Power Drains were identified earlier but one important Power Drain was omitted. There is one power drain that is bigger than any of the other power drains. This eleventh power drain is an organization that wants productivity from its employees without taking some responsibility itself. This creates a disconnect betweeen the organization and its employees. Asking employees continually to do "more with less" is a one-sided relationship that will eventually collapse. If an organization wants to sustain increased productivity, it will have to match the employees' contribution. When the organization does ante up its share, it creates a tremendous Power Boost.

The ELEVENTH Power Drain is an organization that demands increased productivity from its employees but does not match the employees increased contribution with increased rewards.

The organization can contribute its share to creating a more successful work environment by using some combination of these three tools:

Vision Alignment creates a stronger sense of purpose for the individual by aligning the individual's goals with the organization's goals. As the individual works toward the organization's goals, he or she is simultaneously achieving his or her own personal goals.

Valued Behavior Alignment guides the organization in supporting work groups by better understanding the group's values. The organization is then able to put into action policies and programs that supports those values and guides the application of those values to increase alignment between the group and the organization.

Finally, *Action Alignment* improves trust in an organization by aligning action with organization values. Employees can see that espoused values are also the values that are practiced every day. The mission, vision and values statement are not just pretty words on the wall but principles which truly guide decisions.

Vision Alignment

Sam Walton has been quoted as saying that "Capital isn't scarce, vision is." That may be so, but alignment between an individual's vision and an organization's vision is even more scarce. Not many employees see that there can be a relationship between what they want and what the organization is working toward. Audrey, for example, had read her company's mission statement the first week she started her new job. The only reason she read it was because her supervisor said she had to. She didn't pay much attention to it because it was long and used a lot of multi-syllable words. Besides, she was a dishwasher and she didn't think the mission statement had much to do with her job.

Audrey's response to her company's mission statement is typical. The connection between cleaning dishes and her organization's mission statement, "to provide innovative, differentiated, cost-efficient solutions using hardware, software, systems and services and based on energetic, results-oriented employees" wasn't obvious to her. In addition, Audrey's company had given in to a common temptation, the mission statement was written in "intelligentsia." Intelligentsia is the use of multi-syllable words and complex sentence clauses in an effort to impress. When intelligentsia is used, the mission statement may sound like it is very important but the meaning of the mission statement gets lost. It isn't very useful useful as a direction guide if people don't understand it.

Audrey was also under the frequent misconception that the mission statement really only applied to the top management of the organization. A combination of not understanding the mission statement and not seeing how it could apply to her work ensures that the organization's mission statement would not be connected to Audrey's vision for her own future.

Audrey has goals for herself and a vision for her future. The goals and vision are probably not written down but that doesn't mean they don't exist. If you asked Audrey what her goals for the week were, she might list paying her rent, or buying new shoes. If you asked her what her longer term goals were, she might talk about a vacation, going back to school, or moving to a better neighborhood. Audrey is working because there are things that matter to her and working helps her get them.

Chances are that for Audrey, earning money isn't the only purpose for working. Work can also provide:

- a sense of belonging and of being valued;
- relationships;
- growth and challenge;
- enjoyment in the work tasks;
- recognition; and
- a sense of influence and control.

Audrey may not have given much thought to any of these other purposes but one or more are probably influencing her willingness to come to work each

day. Most people work for more than just the pay-
check they receive. When people leave a job, they
almost always leave because one or more of these
other six purposes for work is not being satisfied.
They say they are leaving for better opportunities
or more money, but when they can respond anony-
mously, more money isn't the real reason they left
– they just didn't want to burn any bridges on their
way out!

Audrey may not be consciously aware of what she
wants from a job, but that doesn't change the fact
that a certain percentage of Audrey's energy each
day is directed at satisfying these personal goals.
If Audrey is not able to meet these expectations
through her work, less of her energy will be spent
on organizational tasks and more will be spent on
tasks that help her achieve her personal goals.

Vision Alignment can be illustrated by using a large
arrow to represent the direction the organization
has set through its mission and vision statements
and its strategic plan. The smaller arrows within the
large arrow represent energy spent by an employee
such as Audrey on various tasks throughout a typical week. Some arrows line up perfectly with the
direction set by the goals of the organization. This
happens when the task or activity Audrey is spending energy on is in complete alignment with the
organization's goals. These perfectly vertical arrows
are helping the organization to move ahead. The direction of other arrows are just a little off. Although
they contribute, there is some wasted energy. An
example of this is when Audrey spends a half hour
chatting with another employee. She is not directly
on task but the time spent on this relationship will

contribute to better cooperation and support later. It can indirectly contribute to the organization's goals.

Some arrows are at 90° to the organization's direction. These arrows are not contributing anything. This occurs when Audrey spends 20 minutes talking to her mother on the telephone. The only harm these 90° arrows are doing is that time spent for organizational tasks has been lost.

Finally, some arrows are pointed down. These arrows are working at cross-purposes to the organization's direction. Not only is the organization losing the potential gain, it is also losing actual gains because the negative arrow offsets a positive arrow. This would occur if Audrey was to be sloppy in completing her work and someone else would have to re-wash her dishes. Another example would be if Audrey taught a new employee a "shortcut" to washing dishes that was ineffective or if Audrey began taking food from the kitchen home. In each case, the downward arrow represents actions that work opposite to the organization's goals. In most cases, they will require

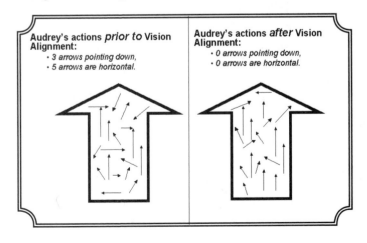

Audrey's actions *prior to* Vision Alignment:
- *3 arrows pointing down,*
- *5 arrows are horizontal.*

Audrey's actions *after* Vision Alignment:
- *0 arrows pointing down,*
- *0 arrows are horizontal.*

someone else to take corrective actions.

If Audrey could see how her work contributed to the organizational goals, her sense of value would improve. If she could see how working on organizational goals would simultaneously help her achieve her own goals, then more of her energy and effort would become aligned with the organization's direction. This would happen automatically because spending energy on what matters to the organization would be the same as spending energy on what mattered to Audrey. Her engagement would automatically increase. As a result, a tremendous boost in energy would be available to the organization.

Creating Vision Alignment

The first step to creating vision alignment is for the organization to have meaningful mission and vision statements. An organization that sets its focus on contributing to the common good offers its employees an opportunity to do something important. Throughout history a common thread in the literature of all cultures is man's search for meaning and purpose. A mission and/or vision statement that sets as its goal the creation of good in the world appeals to that human need for meaning and purpose.

It is beyond the scope of this book to define the difference between mission and vision statements or the process for developing these statements. It is necessary, however, to point out that these statements must be

It is important that an organization's mission and vision statements be written in plain language that is capable of inspiring the heart.

written in simple language so they can be easily re-membered. They also need to be written so that they are capable of inspiring the heart. A lengthy para-graph filled with multi-syllable words isn't going to get the job done.

If the mission and vision statement is hard to read or understand, Audrey won't remember it. If Au-drey doesn't remember it, it cannot inspire her heart or influence her behavior. A statement that can be summarized with a simple "sound byte" is ideal. The test is whether the message can be printed on a t-shirt and read from a distance of 10 feet. For exam-ple, "creating meaningful lives" is the vision of one organization that provides long-term care for peo-ple with developmental disabilities. This is easy to remember and easy to relate to. The true test is that you can stop any employee randomly and ask what the organization's mission is and the employee is able to immediately recite it. You can't get that with a lengthy complicated mission or vision statement and if you can't, it isn't likely the statements are in-fluencing decisions or behavior in the organization.

Writing a mission/vision statement for a social ser-vice organization is easier than for other types of or-ganizations. Making the world better is an obvious part of what they do. The contribution to the greater good of mankind is not as obvious for businesses, but many corporations have still been able to identify how they do contribute. DuPont, primarily a chemi-cal company, has a vision statement that talks about creating solutions that make a "better, safer and healthier life for people." Hewlett-Packard, the com-puter people, has a vision statement that says they "make technical contributions for the advancement and welfare of humanity." For employees, helping an organization accomplish visions like these gives their effort more meaning than just making money for the corporation.

If your organization's mission and vision statements are not inspiring and clear, re-working them is the first step. This is a senior leadership task. If you are not a member of the senior leadership, you can work at raising the issue.

Regardless of senior leadership's response, there is another action you can take to facilitate Vision Alignment. You can lead your work group to develop its own mission and vision statement. These statements should support the organization's statements but can be specific to your work and your work group's role within the organization.

A good mission and vision statement provides direction and influences decisions within the organization. Daveon wasn't sure about a decision he had to make. There was a good argument for either decision he had available. When he asked Conrad, his supervisor, what he should do, Conrad asked him, "Which decision brings us closer to our vision?" That made it easy because only one of the two options

Supervisors can help staff to see the contribution their work makes to accomplishing the organization's mission and vision.

directly supported the vision statement.

Whether it is the organization's mission and vision statements or statements developed for your area, they must be communicated to every employee if they are to have an impact. Framing them and hanging them on the wall, printing them on pens and t-shirts are all common strategies. These strategies are hollow unless there is also a mechanism for allowing these statements to influence decisions.

Having a meaningful mission and vision statement is a good beginning but may not be enough. Some employees may not be able to see the connection between what they do and the organization's vision. The security guard or the cafeteria dishwasher of a pharmaceutical company will probably not see how their work contributes to the vision statement, "creating a healthier world through medicine." As a supervisor, there is a second step that you will need to take. It will be up to you to help your staff make the connection between their work and the organization's vision and mission statement. In the case of the pharmaceutical company, the security guards work of protecting the research facility from vandals and street drug dealers contributes to the company's ability to find new cures. Audrey's work cleaning dishes ensures that research staff are not getting sick after eating in the company's cafeteria. This too, contributes to the company's ability to find new cures.

Vision Alignment is not complete until the individual's own goals have been linked to the organization's goals.

Dayla's staff of six were responsible for entering data into a database that was central to her company's business. Despite Dayla's best efforts at training and simplifying procedures, errors in data entry were well above acceptable levels. In a meeting, Dayla discovered that her staff had no idea how critical the database they maintained was to the success of the business. At the next staff meeting Dayla had a senior manager explain to her staff how reports from the database were used to make a variety of decisions. Their work took on new meaning. They were no longer just entering data. They understood that they were contributing to a critical decision process that could literally make or break the company. Errors went down and surprisingly, attendance improved!

Like Dayla, you may need to help your staff see the value of what they do. All work is important and meaningful but you may have to connect the dots for some staff or they won't see it.

Providing an inspiring mission and vision statement, and helping staff see the value of their own work are good steps but they are not enough. Vision Alignment is not complete until the individuals' own goals have been linked to the organizations' goals.

You can use the tool, *"Aligning Personal Work Needs and Organizational Goals,"* which is on page 103, as an aid to aligning your own needs and then helping your staff align theirs. If you don't already know what your goals are, you can go to Personal Power in Chapter 6 and work on some of the self-awareness strategies suggested there. To align personal goals with organizational goals you will also need a list of your organization's goals. The best place to get these goals is in the most recent copy of your organization's strategic plan.

Once you have your own and your organization's

goals, you are ready to use the tool. To begin, list your organization's goals across the top. On a separate piece of paper, write your own personal work needs and goals for your career, your family, your relationships, etc. Place the needs or goals that are most important to you in the first of the numbered spaces on the lower half of the form, the second in the second space, etc. Rate each goal against the organizational goal based on the degree to which there is overlap between working on the organizational goal and the personal goal. For example, a personal goal for Adelle is to earn a degree in business. A company goal is to promote from within. The overlap between Adelle's goal and her company's goal is near perfect and would score a 4.

Another company goal is to develop new applications for older products. Adelle doesn't see how this matches any of her goals so she gives it a 0. Later, Adelle reviewed the grid with her supervisor, Luke. He pointed out that Adelle's goal to develop her research skills might be useful to helping the organization find new applications for older products. Adelle could see how they matched but it wasn't exactly the kind of research she was interested in so when she changed her score, she gave it a 3 but not a 4.

Once an employee has completed the matrix, the supervisor reviews it with him or her. The easiest ones to discuss are the ones with a direct match (3 or 4). The conversation between the supervisor and the staff member will focus on these direct matches, looking for ways to help the employee to spend a reasonable percent of his or her week on tasks associated with goals that matched up well. If it is possible to realign tasks it is well worth the effort.

While discussing solid matches is useful, the more interesting discussions will occur around the poorer matches. With some creativity, you may be able to adjust a task or goal to improve the match. Latrice had a personal career goal to become a lawyer. Her current position was as an office administrator. Her organization had a goal to secure another government contract. Latrice scored herself a 2 on the match between her goal and this organizational goal because she occasionally helped to produce progress reports on other government contracts. Mandy, her supervisor, suggested that Latrice take a three-day workshop that taught basic legal terminology to non-professionals. Mandy also assigned Latrice to a committee that was working on a government Requests For Proposals (RFP's). Latrice changed her score from a 2 to a 5.

With a deeper understanding that comes through discussion, you may be able to help your staff see new possibilities in the organizational objectives. Cheyenne had taken a course in Organization Development (OD) last semester and it made such an impression, she made a career goal to become an internal OD consultant. Her workgroup had developed its own strategic plan and a goal in the plan was to reduce errors. Cheyenne scored a 0 on the match between her OD consultant goal and this goal. Her supervisor, Terry pointed out that the errors were a performance issue. Data analysis tools she had learned as part of her course would be helpful in diagnosing the source of the problem. Cheyenne could then see that if she was to work on reducing errors, there would be a perfect match between her

Aligning Personal Work Needs and Organizational Goals

	Organization Goals						Total
4 = **Perfect Match** *(Working toward organization goal allows you to **fully satisfy** the indicator need)*							
3 = **Good Match** *(Working toward organization goal allows you to **satisfy most** of the indicator need)*							
2 = **Somewhat Matches** *(Working toward organization goal allows you to **satisfy some** of the indicator need)*							
1 = **Very Poor Match** *(Working toward organization goal allows you to **satisfy very little** of the indicator need)*							
0 = No match at all							
Personal Work Needs							**Total**
1.							
2.							
3.							
4.							
5.							
6.							
Total							

goal and the organizational goal.

Consequences of Vision Alignment

To achieve Vision Alignment you have ensured that your mission and vision statement is clear and inspiring. You have also helped your staff understand the importance of their work and how their work supports the mission and vision of the organization. Finally, you have helped your staff improve the connection between their own goals with the or-

Vision Alignment
- *Inspiring mission and vision statement*
- *Recognition of each person's contribution to mission and vision*
- *Individual alignment of personal goals with organizational goals.*

ganization's goals. When an employee's vision is aligned with the organization's, he or she is enjoying the work more because there is more in it for him or her. The result of this will be a major boost because much less energy will be spent on avoidance or escape behaviors. Vision Alignment has produced a major power boost because employees are happier and more productive and more engaged!

Valued Behavior Alignment

Vision Alignment focused on helping staff align with the organization's direction. Now it's time for the organization to return the favor and do some work on aligning its actions to employees values. Valued Behavior Alignment focuses on the values at the core of a work group that are influencing the behavior of the group. With knowledge of these valued behaviors, the organization can respond in a way that demonstrates support and respect for these values.

A lot has been written about organizational culture and its influence on both beliefs and behaviors of its members. While an organization's culture is important, group sub-cultures influence values, beliefs and behavior more significantly. This is because the sub-culture or group culture surrounds the individual all day, every day. It exists because it offers its members *Group culture influences behavior more than the organizational culture because the group culture surrounds members all day, every day.* identity within the larger organization and provides solutions to problems in the immediate work environment.

It is believed that the sub-culture reflects the larger organizational culture. Trainers who deal with teams or work groups from various parts of an organization might not agree with that statement. Their experience is more likely to have taught them that every group takes on its own unique personality. That group personality heavily influences the behavior of the group members.

Randy was the director of the training department and as part of an organizational development program, he did a study of seventeen self-directed work teams in his organization. In this study, the Bar-On EQi (Stein & Book, 2000) was used to create a group profile across fifteen emotional intelligence competencies. All seventeen teams hired new members from the same applicant pool, they all did the same kind of work and they all received the same training.

Despite having so many things in common, Randy was surprised to find that not one of the seventeen teams had the same emotional intelligence profile as any other team, even though the average overall EQi scores were not significantly different. Some teams put a premium on assertive and independent behavior while other teams emphasized interpersonal relationships or social responsibility, etc.

This variation in emotional intelligence profiles between the groups is not a surprising finding. Groups that work together develop their own sub-culture which influences expectations, beliefs, rituals and behavior. This sub-culture is a reflection of a set of values that the group has come to accept. These values drive behavior and influence its members' perceptions. The group values are defended and enforced. They influence what the group will determine as acceptable behavior and what is unacceptable.

Understanding just how different groups within the same organization can be from one another is important because what will serve to motivate one group can do the opposite for another. Manuel's experience with two teams he supervised is an example of this. The first team, Jalene's team, prided itself on punctuality and attendance. They once went 163 days without a single person being absent or late. The streak was finally ended when Lorne broke his leg and couldn't drive to work.

The second team, Ron's team, was rather free spirited. Ron had learned that the team could be very creative if he gave them a free hand. Folks came to work late and left early but the job always got done so Ron turned a blind eye to their attendance behavior. When Manuel had a tough assignment, he liked to give it to Ron's team because they would always find a way to get the job done.

Manuel wanted to reward both Jalene's and Ron's team for consistently meeting quotas. He announced that as a reward, he was going to officially institute a flexible schedule. While this was a wonderful strategy for encouraging productivity with Ron's team, it was exactly contrary to what Jalene's team expected from each other. Such a "reward" was likely to cause stress for Jalene's team because they would be forced to renegotiate their group expectations.

Group culture values determines what behavior is acceptable and unacceptable.

Jalene's and Ron's team are at extreme ends of a continuum but they illustrate the point. When a "one-size fits-all" approach to improving productivity is taken, the results will be uneven, depending on the variations between the groups. Of more concern is that what was intended as a benevolent act may be experienced by some groups as very unpleasant.

Knowing the valued behaviors of a group gives the organization an opportunity to demonstrate respect for its members by adjusting demands and rewards to support those behaviors. By making adjustments this way, the organization minimizes resistance to change. The organization can now make use of the natural energy to achieve its goals. This is much like a sailboat using the wind instead of fighting it.

The challenge is to know what the valued behaviors are. If you simply ask the members of the group what it values and therefore what influences its behavior, the group may give you a response but it is unlikely to be right. It is more likely to be a description of what the group aspires to value or what the group thinks it should value. The values that are actually influencing the group's behavior are so much a part of the group they are taken for granted. It's like asking a fish to discover water! That makes it difficult. Fortunately, there is a tool that can help with this, the VBA discussed in Chapter 3. This tool is part of a Triangulated Analysis. It helps the group reach down to its collective unconscious to identify its core valued behaviors. A description of the steps for implementing the VBA is on pages 48 and 49.

Once a supervisor knows what underlying valued behaviors are influencing the group, respectfully reinforcing is much easier to do. Many books have been published on how to motivate staff. The result is a confusing inventory of strategies. Almost all of these strategies have been successful under at least some circumstances. Supervisors seeking to improve productivity will apply the strategy "du jour" and may or may not get the intended results. Once you understand that groups develop a value system, the explanation for the uneven results becomes apparent. Unless the reinforcing strategy happens to complement the values of the group, it will have, at best, neutral results. More frequently, the strategy will be interpreted negatively by the group and will contribute to cynicism and/or demoralization.

Julia was the lead member of a very supportive team. Over time they had developed an "us vs. the world" attitude that worked for them. Turnover was low and their productivity was consistently on target. Visitors from the main office visited the department one day and they apparently liked what they saw. At the next all-staff meeting Julia's supervisor publicly congratulated her. Julia's team members teased her about "going over to the dark side" and asking her if she could still hang out with the "common folks." Julia knew that it wasn't just teasing, the team was angry with her. That was the beginning of tension between team members that lasted several months. Unfortunately for many organizations, they implement a strategy like Julia's company did with the best of intentions to recognize and encourage a staff member but get the opposite of what they want because their strategy contradicts group values.

Pages 85-87 lists potential strategies for respectfully reinforcing. The list, by itself, is not very helpful but, when coupled with the information produced by the Valued Behavior Assessment, it is a gold mine. For example, a group that values learning would appreciate opportunities for training whereas another group might dread being sent for training. A group that is competitive will enjoy challenging another work group to reduce error rates. An innovative team would appreciate a tough problem to solve. Clearly, there are different strokes for different folks. Instead of *The VBA will allow you to accurately predict how your work group will respond to a proposed change.* blindly applying a motivational strategy or choosing a motivational strategy based on what a supervisor personally finds motivating, the strategy can be carefully targeted to what will be most effective for the group.

The strength of the Valued Behavior Assessment goes beyond just respectfully rein-forcing the group. It also allows you, as the supervisor, to predict with ac-curacy how any change is likely to be responded to by the group. Instead of introducing a change, hop-ing for the best and dealing with any resistance after it emerges, you can be proactive. You can anticipate what resistance is likely to emerge and make adjust-ments to minimize it beforehand. A stitch in time saves nine and where resistance to change is con-cerned, this is doubly applicable. Small things can have big effects. A small adjustment can save a lot of wasted energy for your staff, for you and for the organization.

Attempts at motivating a group will be ineffective unless the motivator happens to complement the values of the group.

Jeremy's team has a lot of fun at work. The team worked hard and with the pressure to be creative in time to meet deadlines, there is a lot of stress. The break room is a noisy, great place for a mental break. Jeremy knew that the re-organization of the offices being planned was going to eliminate the break room. Before the re-organization occurred he warned his team of the coming change and sug-gested they brainstorm an alternative location for a meeting area. They came up with a great option that met their need and used a space that would other-wise have been wasted. An adjustment was easily made to the floor plans to accommodate the groups need for a location to decompress.

Using the Valued Behavior Assessment will allow you to harness the power within the group. It is a small investment of time but it delivers a large return. Understanding your staff better and working with them instead of at cross-purposes, demonstrates respect and builds trust.

Valued Behavior Alignment requires creativity and often a level of organizational flexibility to implement. The resulting power boost is, however, significant. The employee will be more engaged and as a result there will be a major boost in both productivity AND morale for the organization.

Action Alignment

The third component of the power boost is Action Alignment. This third component is a reality test. Is the organization's perception of its values grounded in practice? Is the organization living out its values or is it paying lip service to them? Lip-service to values has the potential to drain energy quickly. Members of the organization will easily identify inconsistencies between what is said and what is actually done. Once detected, trust is damaged and once damaged, it is difficult to re-build.

Aligning organizational actions with a groups valued behaviors is a small investment of time but it delivers a major return in productivity and morale.

Anna's previous employer was building a new office facility. Her friend Heather worked in another department. Heather's entire department was sent to look at the new location. When they returned they were greeted with lay-off notices on their desks. This was a nasty way of informing employees of a lay-off. As bad as it was for those who were laid off, the impact on those who were left behind was just as bad. Lay-offs may be inevitable, but in an organization that professes to value its employees, the way this lay-off was implemented was in complete contradiction to its espoused values. If downsizing is the only option, dealing with those who are being laid-off honestly and fairly is as much for the employees leaving as for those staying.

It is easy to announce and live out values such as "Employees are our number one asset." It is when times are not good that the truth emerges. Under these circumstances, what actions does leadership take? Greenwood Industries referred to itself as a "learning organization" and held as a high value continuous improvement. When the economy had a downturn, employees thought the budget for training and tuition reimbursement would be cut. Instead, senior management opted for a pay cut for themselves and they kept several middle management positions vacant until the economy improved. Greenwood Industries senior managers made some tough decisions and made the first sacrifices. The choices they made spoke louder than any sign on the wall about the values of the organization.

Contrast this with Redwood Industries. When Redwood Industries ran into financial trouble, the senior managers argued to the union that unless the union made some concessions, the company was going to go under. The union agreed to accept a pay cut to save jobs for its membership. A month after the new contract was signed, the senior managers were all given very large bonuses for their handling of the crisis. Not surprisingly, union members walked off the job when they heard about the bonuses.

Redwood is an obvious example of an organization not living up to its words and as expected, trust was damaged. Trust can be eroded through more subtle inconsistencies as well. Surveys conducted and feedback from the survey never shared with the participants leaves them feeling used or ignored. Worse than that is asking for input AFTER decisions have been made.

Racine was re-organizing her department of forty staff. Functions were being shifted so that some people were gaining new responsibilities and span of control and others were losing responsibilities. The moves included Lawrence, a supervisor Racine had counseled for poor performance. Before implementing changes, Racine reviewed them *As in any relationship, once trust in the organization is damaged, it is very difficult to re-build.* with J.J., the head of Human Resources. Concerned that Lawrence might complain that the change was because Racine "had it in for him" J.J. insisted Racine survey her staff about skills and work preferences before announcing the change. J.J. explained, "That way you can say that you are making these changes based on the survey and no one can complain it's personal." The point of the survey was strictly for appearances because the decisions had already been made. It doesn't take long for employees to figure out when the request for their input is a sham. When they do, the disrespect inherent to being misled will have long-term negative effects.

Another example, less deliberate, is the organization that announces a new initiative, insisting everyone participate but doesn't follow through with any action. Gino's company announced a "High Performance Organization" initiative. He wasn't sure what that meant but he knew he would soon find out. He and his department were scheduled to attend a two-day workshop to learn about it and how to implement it with his group. Gino was dealing with the end of year reports and wasn't excited about taking two days away from work. It would mean a lot of evening and weekend work to catch up because the deadlines for his reports could not be adjusted. Attendance at the workshop was mandatory so he reluctantly attended. Six months later Gino could see no evidence that the concepts taught during the workshop had been applied within the organization. People used some of the language from the workshop but there wasn't any other sign of a High Performance Organization. More then that, senior management were now talking about implementing still another initiative.

Once trust in the organization is damaged, it is very difficult to re-build.

Gino is developing a degree of cynicism regarding senior management's leadership. From Gino's perspective, they have demonstrated a lack of respect for his time and priorities and poor judgement and execution of organizational development strategies. This cynicism can easily shift to a "why should I care" attitude, because from Gino's perspective management didn't care about his workload or deadlines.

Gino is losing faith in the leadership of his organization and disengagement won't be far behind.

A proactive way of ensuring that Action Alignment occurs is through the use of individual development plans. Ethan had recently joined the company and was impressed that one of the first things his new supervisor did was to work out a development plan for him. This was a major difference from the haphazard way Ethan had experienced training and development opportunities in the past. Based on his development plan, Ethan was confident that he could work on his personal career goals and in doing so, he could also see how the organization would benefit. He learned from his supervisor that using personal development plans was part of a strategic action the organization was using to create a competitive edge. That sounded a lot different than anything Ethan had heard before! Ethan could see that he was an important part of the organization's future.

Action Alignment is not easy for organizations to do. Decisions are made based on multiple criteria. What appears to be reasonable and consistent in the boardroom can look very different to others who do not have the benefit of the full context in which the decision was made. Disengagement due to misalignment can become an insidious intruder. An organization's leaders need to watch for inconsistencies between its professed values and its behaviors. This vigilance, however, is probably not going to be enough because the vantage point of the board-room does not provide the same view as the rest of the organization may have. Tools that measure engagement can offer an important avenue for feedback. Using the Vision Exam on page 50 is an excellent tool for gathering information regarding staff perceptions of the decisions and behavior of an organization's leadership team. With information from tools such as these, managers and supervisors can make adjustments and corrections early that provide employees with evidence that they are important and that the organization intends to live out its values.

Creating Win-Win-Wins

Power Boosts provide the opportunity for shared responsibility for a win-win-win. Aligning Actions removes mistrust and loss of faith in the organization. Mistrust and loss of faith are big barriers to achieving high morale and productivity. Valued Behavior Alignment helps the organization support the valued behaviors of its work groups and teams. Vision Alignment helps the employee satisfy some personal goals through contributions to organizational goals. Individually, Vision, Valued Behavior and Actions Alignment will each make a difference. Combine them and you have an exponential change, you have a Power Boost of significant proportion and an increase in work engagement.

> *"The achievement of an organization are the results of the combined effort of each individual."*
> Vince Lombardi

Chapter 6

Personal Power

"...be the change..."
Mahatma Gandhi

Personal Power focuses on taking control of your career and building your own work engagement. That's a good news – bad news scenario. The good news is that you *can* take control. The bad news is that if you want to be more engaged in your work, you may have to do it yourself. This chapter is for you, the individual employee, and it is for supervisors who would like to help their employees help themselves.

One word of caution to supervisors. If there are serious Power Drains present or need for work on organizational Power Boosts, you do not want to introduce Personal Power concepts to your staff. They are not likely to respond well to such a move because, from their perspective, the organization is not doing its share of the work. Personal Power focuses on personal change. That's an excellent step but the individual employee is going to want to see that his or her employer is a partner in the change. Otherwise it will feel as if the employer is not taking any responsibility. It all goes back to the unwritten psychological contract. Employees expect to get from their employers a fair return for what they give to their employers. So, for your employees to respond well to your teaching them ways to get more out of their work, they are going to want to see that the organization is going to do its share of the work as well.

The time is always right to work on Personal Power if it is something you have found independent of your employer. In that case it is a personal commitment made to yourself, for yourself. The dynamics are very different and so, if you are a supervisor, you can still make good use of Personal Power, even if the time is not right to share it with your staff. In fact, having worked with Personal Power tools yourself will make it much easier to teach them to staff. Your staff may notice changes in you and ask about them. That is an excellent opportunity to share Personal Power and under this condition, it is likely to be quite positively received.

If you aren't feeling fully engaged at work, you have two immediate choices, stay or leave. There are circumstances when leaving is truly the most prudent choice but beware of its seductiveness. More often you will do better if you stay. Other pastures are rarely as green as they appear

You do NOT have to resign yourself to a boring, frustrating or unfair situation just because you don't want to leave or you can't leave your current employer.

and while the novelty of a new job is exciting in the short-term, it also brings with it some tremendous stress. Putting the stress aside, there is a nasty secret that career counselors and therapists know: the new job usually has the same problems you just left in the old job.

The reason the new job usually has the same problems as the old one is because you are still the same person. How you react to things stays the same. That means you will seek out certain conditions or re-create conditions that ultimately lead to the same pattern of issues. The difference is that in the new job, you have lost the benefit of the social capital you built through relationships at your old job. This is a major loss, so be careful about moving too quickly to change jobs.

Deidre worked for a large law firm and supervised the administrative staff. This was a senior position but, in this organization, she had reached the top of her ladder and she felt unappreciated by the professional staff. She looked around and found a great alternative. Two years into the new job, Deidre recognized that some responsibilities and tasks had changed but she was still working in a situation that treated professional staff with more status. She had very limited influence on the organization despite being a member of the leadership team. Changing jobs had meant leaving behind her best friend and ten years of job tenure. Deidre seriously questioned whether starting over was really worth what she had lost. Deidre's situation is not unusual. There is a price when you change employers. In some situations it is worth the price but be sure you understand what the price is.

So, what if you have decided you don't want to leave your current job or worse yet, you can't leave your current job? Does that mean you need to accept a boring, frustrating or unfair situation? If you feel unrecognized and under-utilized do you have to resign yourself to the situation? Well of course the answer is no, there is always something you can do. Dr. Donald Baer, a Professor Emeritus at the University of Kansas, used to tell his students, *"you can have what you want, or you can have your excuses, it's all about choices."* He explained his comment by pointing out he would love a bigger sail boat but he was fond of keeping his home. Instead of buying the sailboat he was making his mortgage payments. The key is to understand that it was **his choice** to pass on the boat. That meant he was in control. He understood his priorities and was consciously choosing. You need to know what you want and then make sure your behavior is moving you towards achieving your goals.

That's a lot easier said than done. Wayne's department was re-organized and he was no longer a supervisor. He felt humiliated and wanted to quit but he was only three years away from a full retirement. Financially, it didn't make sense to *Building your work engagement will improve your own personal quality of life.* quit but he hated the work that was now his job. Wayne does have choices, he can be miserable for a long three years or the last three years can be his best three years. Whether he recognizes it or not, the choice is up to him. The first step to a better experience is for Wayne to decide he wants things to be better and to recognize he is in the driver's seat. If he wants to be a victim, he certainly has just cause but the price is a long three years before he can escape to retirement. The alternative is taking control and creating a different reality. This chapter will point the way. It's up to Wayne and it's also up to you. It would be wonderful if your organization addressed the power drains or implemented power boosts but even if it doesn't, you can still be more engaged if you choose to be.

Why Build Personal Power?

There are many things you can do to help yourself and to increase your work engagement. The question is: why should you? This is a particularly important question if your trust in your organization has been shaken. If you no longer feel that your organization is going to treat you fairly, why should you put in an effort to becoming more engaged? The answer is easy, because you aren't going to work at being more engaged for your employer, you are doing it for yourself. Yes, if you increase your engagement your employer will certainly benefit but YOU will benefit MORE.

How do you benefit? To begin with, you spend at least forty of your prime waking hours at work. Your family and friends get your left-over hours. You are spending a major chunk of your life working, what would it do to your overall quality of life if those forty hours were stimulating, energizing and enjoyable? Owen prided himself in his ability "to leave the office at the office." When he left to go home he blocked all thoughts of work until he arrived at work the next day. He was very good at it and thought that this protected his family from the frustration and boredom he felt at work. The problem is, Owen didn't really leave his work at work. The emotions rolling around in his gut still went home with him. Owen struggled with insomnia and digestive problems. He was taking medication for depression and things at home were often tense. What Owen didn't realize was that it is impossible to leave the office at the office. Emotions stirred at the office infiltrate his perceptions of everything else that happens. How much better would it be for Owen if the emotions at work stirred feelings of self-confidence, being valued, excitement, eagerness, curiosity, fascination, stimulation, etc.?

There is evidence that high engagement is correlated with better health and happier personal relationships (Crabtree, 2005; Gallup, 2005). That shouldn't be a surprise. People who are highly engaged are as stressed as those who are unengaged or disengaged. The difference is that people with high engagement feel in control of their lives and so the stress is "eustress." Eustress is a healthy stress because it contributes to your feeling fulfilled. It generates energy, creativity, and self-worth.

The unengaged or disengaged are feeling trapped by their situation. This helplessness makes their stress a "distress" and this is deadly. Distress puts the body on high alert and the body's auto-immune system is activated. Adrenaline is pumping to prepare the body for "fight or flight" and all other systems in the body are put on hold until the crisis passes. The problem is that with a job that leaves you unengaged or disengaged, the crisis rarely passes. Your system is on some level of alert forty hours a week. Exhausted, you go home with little reserve for coping with anything happening there. Live like this, week after week, and your body and relationships are going to wear out. The "fight or flight" response is important to survival, but when it is left on for long periods of time, it's like revving your car for extended periods, it is going to break down!

Two kinds of Stress:

Eustress
Stimulating, energizing. Contributes to feeling fulfilled.

Distress
Tense, anxious, on high alert. Feelings of helplessness.

So, are you convinced? Improving your work engagement is for YOU. Yes, your employer benefits but you benefit more! So, how do you improve your personal work engagement?

Money vs. Work Engagement

Before strategies for improving your work engagement can be explored, the issue of money has to be addressed. The old adage, "money can't buy happiness" is oftened followed with "but it sure helps!" There are always places to put more money but if you are dealing with a situation in which you can't pay your rent or mortgage or you can't buy food or medicine for your family, money is your priority goal. This goes back to Maslow's Heirarchy of Needs (1962). You have to meet your basic survival needs before higher order needs for relationships or self-

actualization become important. If you aren't earning enough to ensure your basic needs, it is possible
to still be engaged. Spiritual leaders and devoted
craftsmen are examples of this. But, if you are not
meeting your basic needs and you are not engaged,
becoming more engaged is not your first priority. In
this situation, making money is much more important than improving your work engagement.

There is one more situation in which money is still an
issue. If your earnings are well below the market
rate then, unless some-
thing is done to remedy
this situation, increas-
ing engagement will be
difficult. The reason for
this is that being serious-
ly underpaid will, in most cases, create a Fairness
Power Drain. This power drain will undermine your
organizational affinity. The exception to this is when
the lack of income is compensated through work relationships and vision and action alignments. If the
leaders of your organization are working as hard
as you are and are sacrificing personal income to
achieve valued organizational goals, then the fairness power drain is minimized and your *organizational affinity* is not at risk.

> *Working with purpose
> goes much deeper,
> lasts longer and
> matters more than
> money.*

Setting aside these two situations, just increasing
your income will not increase your engagement.
Engagement is more than money, it's working with
"purpose." It goes much deeper and therefore, lasts
longer and matters more than money. It's also true
that if you are highly engaged you are more likely
to be considered for promotion. It couldn't be otherwise. If you are committed to, and energized by

your work you are going to be shooting for excellence because it matters to you. Creativity, problem-solving, risk-taking, initiative and dedication are all a part of excellence that make you a good candidate for bonuses, promotion, and success. The point is, your focus is on excellence and success is a natural and pleasant side-effect. When you work toward increasing your engagement instead of your income, you will often get your cake and get to eat it too!

Avenues for Building Personal Power

How do you increase your personal power for work engagement? That's not an easy question to answer because there are at least ten avenues and you are the only one who can know which avenue is right for you. In fact, routes to work engagement that are not right for you might look too simple or even silly or useless. Only those avenues that match your needs, your comfort zone and your circumstances are going to look reasonable to you. Given that, you will

Finding the right avenue for you is worth the effort. Dramatic change can happen and the result will spill over to a general improvement in quality of life.

need to be patient as you wade through the rough roads to find the right avenue for you. It is worth the effort, however, because once you have identified the right avenue and the appropriate strategies, dramatic change can happen. The result will spill over from your career to a general improvement in your quality of life.

The ten avenues available for building Personal Power are:

1. *Know Yourself*

The focus of this avenue is on understanding what matters most to you, what you enjoy doing, and what your strengths are. If what you spend forty hours a week doing is something you enjoy and you are good at, you will naturally be more successful. This avenue includes identifying your future and planning a route to achieve that future.

2. *Remove the Emotional Blocks*

This is similar to Know Yourself but goes a little deeper. This avenue challenges you to examine the fears and beliefs that are getting in your way and to build new, more useful responses. If you are up to the challenge of dealing with these familiar fears and excuses, changes made in this avenue can have a tremendous impact.

3. *Connect with Others*

Two heads are better than one and the right team is even better. You don't have to build your career on your own. This avenue helps you find ways to make use of the talents and resources that are all around you.

4. *Take Action*

Keeping busy puts you in position to see opportunities that may have been hidden. In addition, the stimulation of worthwhile activity will help your brain produce the endorphins that are responsible for feeling good about life. This avenue is focused on finding the kinds of activities that will stave off boredom, create new experiences or give you a sense of control over your environment.

5. Re-focus Your Thinking

What you think affects how you feel and how you behave. It also affects your non-verbal behavior which sends a signal to others about how they should treat you. This avenue addresses what is going in your head and provides you with a variety of strategies for changing how you feel about things, how you respond to others, and how others are responding to you.

6. Improve Your Skills

Learning is a major contributor to quality of life. Learning gives us more control over our environments and makes more opportunities available to us. This avenue is focused on the many strategies available to you to increase your work skills and to make yourself more valuable and to your organization AND more marketable.

7. Help Others

You are not alone and helping others not only feels good, it helps you too. This avenue explores strategies for reaching out to help someone else. Helping others and knowing you have done a good thing stimulates the brain to produce those endorphins you need to feel good about life. With an increased level of endorphins comes a new and clearer perspective on your own situation.

8. Get Healthy

This avenue is focused on taking care of yourself physically. It is easy to get caught up in the urgency of deadlines and lose sight of taking care of the machine, your body, you depend on most. With good health you get more done and feel better about what you do. This avenue is about making yourself and your own physical needs a priority.

9. Reward Yourself

You put a lot of expectations on yourself and you are probably like most people and pretty hard on yourself when you don't measure up. That would be fine if you also congratulated yourself and made sure you took some time for fun but this often gets lost in the shuffle of meeting deadlines. This avenue provides strategies for ensuring that you treat yourself as well as you treat others.

10. Be Clear

Winston Churchill is said to have stated that the biggest barrier to communication between the English and the Americans in WWII was that they "thought" they spoke the same language. The problem with thinking we understand the words another uses is a problem that is rampant in organizations. This avenue is focused on strategies for helping you to be more effective in your ability to influence the actions of others.

Building
Personal Power

The first step to building Personal Power is to identify the avenue or avenues that are going to be most useful to you. To help you find the most appropriate match, you can complete the Personal Power Direction Tool found on page 133. Once you have done so, you can look at the avenues that are best suited to your needs and interests. The avenues and the strategies associated with each are discussed in detail in Appendix IV.

The Personal Power Direction Tool will help you to identify which of the possible ten avenues will be your quickest route to building work engagement. Each avenue consists of several strategies. It is outside the scope of this chapter to provide detailed explanations on how to implement each strategy. A full explanation of each strategy and exercises for implementing them are available in the *Personal Power for Work Engagement Fieldbook (Daoust & Eubank, in publication)*. The self-help section of your local library or bookstore will also be a rich resource for information about the strategies associated with your recommended avenue(s).

Personal Power means that you are taking control of your own engagement. You are actively improving your own *Personal Power allows you to make the forty hours a week you spend at work more meaningful to you.* quality of life by making the forty hours you spend at work more meaningful. Personal Power is focused on giving you a reason to look forward to

your day when you get up each morning. The pages
of suggestions that are provided in Appendix IV are
just the beginning. There are a wealth of strategies
that can help you find more personal value in your
work and that, by
itself, presents a
problem for many
people. They go to
the bookstore or
the library and are
confronted with an
overwhelming number of self-help books, all prom-
ising that they have the answer. Every week more
titles are published and the confusion gets bigger.

*You need to identify avenues
that are most appropriate to
you AND prioritize your focus
based on which avenues will
provide the biggest positive
outcome.*

The Personal Power Direction Tool (PPDT) will help
you zero in on your highest priorities. Once you
have, you will be able to go directly to those self-help
resources that will make the biggest, most meanin-
gul difference for you.

Building Tips

Once you have identified which strategies or mix of
strategies you want to implement, there are a few
tips that will make your efforts more successful.

1. Tell someone you trust what you are doing. You
    will be more committed to your effort if you have
    admitted out loud that you are taking action. In
    addition, having someone who will support you
    in your effort will make it easier to stay with it
    when your own commitment wavers.

2. Write an action plan, breaking out the steps and

dates for completion. Writing the plan on paper will make it more real. We are more likely to follow through on a commitment that we have taken the time to write. You will remember the steps better if you have seen them on paper and there is something about seeing them in black and white makes them feel more real.

3. Set reasonable goals, actively changing one thing at a time. If you decide you want to quit smoking, lose weight and get more exercise, do them one at a time. Don't tackle them all at once. Too much change all at once will be overwhelming.

4. Don't look up the mountain. Once you have a plan, focus on the step you are taking and the next step. If you look at how far you have to go, you will risk overwhelming yourself.

5. Do look DOWN the mountain. Take time to look over how far you have come. One step isn't very far but added to the step before it and the step before that, they all add up. If you don't take time to look back you can overlook how much progress you have made and become unnecessarily discouraged.

One Last Word on Personal Power

Personal Power is for you, not your employer. Your employer may benefit but that is a side-effect, not the goal. Effort put towards developing your Personal Power may lead you to a different employer or a different career or it may deepen your commitment to your current employer or career. You may make changes that increase your income, status, or responsibilities or the changes you make could do exactly the opposite. Regardless, the changes you make will improve your quality of life by helping you to use your time in a more meaningful way. That is a true definition of success!

"The unexamined life is not worth living"

Plato

Instructions for Scoring the Personal Power Direction Tool

- *Transfer your scores on the PPDT to the scoresheet by filling the corresponding number of squares in the column as the score for the questions listed.*
  (For example, if you circled a 3 on Question 7, fill in squares 1-3 in the "Know Yourself" column. Then if you scored a 2 on Question 15, fill in squares 4-5 in the same column. Finally, for your score of 5 on Question 28, fill in squares 6-10. This height of the bar and associated score indicates that strategies associated with Know Yourself, described in Appendix IV have an immediate priority for improving your engagement.)

- *Complete scoring for all 10 Avenues for Building Personal Power and begin action with the ones that have the lowest final scores as indicated by the height of the column bars.*

Personal Power Direction Tool

Circle the number that best represents your response to each statement.

Completely Agree = 5   Sort of Agree = 4
Neither Agree nor Disagree = 3
Sort of Disagree = 2   Completely Disagree = 1

1.	In the last year, my relationships at work have increased in quality or quantity.	5 4 3 2 1
2.	I have the skills and training to do other interesting jobs in this organization.	5 4 3 2 1
3.	At work, I am very good at reading people's feelings.	5 4 3 2 1
4.	I frequently praise others at work.	5 4 3 2 1
5.	I have learned something interesting or useful when I was helping someone else.	5 4 3 2 1
6.	At work, when I am asked to take on something new, I know I will be successful.	5 4 3 2 1
7.	I have a clear sense of what kind of work fits me best.	5 4 3 2 1
8.	At work, I can take control of things that happen to me.	5 4 3 2 1
9.	I am better able to do my job now than I was a year ago.	5 4 3 2 1
10.	My work challenges me.	5 4 3 2 1
11.	At work, I am comfortable speaking for something I believe in.	5 4 3 2 1
12.	I have the energy to do my job.	5 4 3 2 1
13.	I reward myself for a job well done.	5 4 3 2 1
14.	When something is difficult at work, I can get helpful advice from someone.	5 4 3 2 1
15.	I have a clear sense of the direction I want to take my career.	5 4 3 2 1
16.	At work, I get things done every day.	5 4 3 2 1
17.	At work, I am flexible in my approach to things.	5 4 3 2 1
18.	In the last year, I have frequently helped others at work.	5 4 3 2 1
19.	In the last year, I have taken five or less sick days.	5 4 3 2 1
20.	Parts of my work day are fun!	5 4 3 2 1
21.	If I see something that needs to be done, I do it!	5 4 3 2 1
22.	It is easy for me to try something new at work.	5 4 3 2 1
23.	I regularly exchange work-related information with others at work.	5 4 3 2 1
24.	In the last year, my skills and/or job knowledge have increased.	5 4 3 2 1
25.	When I speak, people will listen to my point of view.	5 4 3 2 1
26.	When I am at work, I enjoy being there.	5 4 3 2 1
27.	At work, I take an optimistic attitude.	5 4 3 2 1
28.	I have a clear sense of purpose in my life.	5 4 3 2 1
29.	At work, when I have had an idea, I get started implementing it immediately.	5 4 3 2 1
30.	Laughter is often heard at work.	5 4 3 2 1

Personal Power Direction Tool
Scoring Sheet

	Know Yourself	Remove Emotional Blocks	Connect With Others	Take Action	Refocus Your Thinking	Advance Your Skills	Help Others	Get Healthy	Be Kind to Yourself	Be Clear
Questions	7 15 28	8 22 29	1 14 23	10 16 21	6 17 27	2 9 24	4 5 18	12 19 26	13 20 30	3 11 25

Low Priority Avenue: 15, 14, 13, 12

Intermediate Priority Avenues: 11, 10, 9, 8, 7

Highest Priority Avenues: 6, 5, 4, 3, 2, 1

Chapter 7

Putting it all Together

"The whole is greater than the sum of its parts."
Unknown

The Co-generating System model consists of three major components: Triangulated Analysis, Power of Three and Change Momentum as presented in Chapter 2. The first two components have been dis-

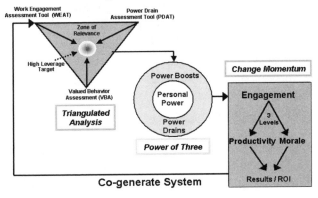

cussed. The potential for Change Momentum is created by combining the first two components and is the topic of this chapter.

The Triangulated Analysis identifies appropriate focal points and provides a road map for selecting strategies. The Power of Three guides your selection of change strategies from a myriad of organizational development options described in the lit-

The Co-generate System combines three old organizational development ideas in a unique way that creates a new and synergistic approach to change.

erature. The strength of the Power of Three is that it knits strategies together to create an approach that involves all levels of the organization in a targeted, efficient approach to creating a sustainable change. This strategic blending of tools creates the Change Momentum.

Doing an assessment before implementing a change effort is an approach that is well documented as a critical first step to a change effort in any organization development textbook. Combining several tools for creating change is also not a new concept. Nor is the idea of involving several levels of the organization in the change process anything new. It is the way in which the Co-generate System pulls these three older ideas together that creates a new, synergistic approach.

While textbooks and various authors recommend specific targeting, they haven't been very helpful in explaining how to do it. Triangulated Analysis gives you quick and easy to use tools that produce a previously unavailable level of precision. Combine this level of precision with the Power of Three and a major source of synergy is created. The Triangulated Analysis identifies **specific** and **unique** targets for *each* level in the organization: the individual, the group and work environment, and the organizational strategic/ cultural level.

Working at any one level or with any one tool offered by the organizational development literature can create change. It will be slow, tenuous or vulnerable to the push-back (a.k.a. resistance to change) of a system re-asserting its status quo. With the Co-generate System, change is faster and sustainable because there are more avenues being traveled by more participants who are all headed in the same direction. The Triangulated Analysis identifies the best leverage point for change strategies at EACH level of the organization. Many tools can be used to achieve a variety of results that all support each other. Resistance to change is minimized because change is owned at every level of the organization. It is simultaneously a bottom-up and top-down change process. Changes at one level are integrated into the changes occurring at another level, in real-time. Despite the change occurring throughout the organization, the stress of chaos is minimized because all change is directed toward the same target: simultaneous increases in productivity and morale.

Resistance to change is really, at its core, resistance to threat. People rarely resist a change that has obvious benefits for them. Proof of that is the frequency with which lottery winners turn down their winnings based on a fear of change. We know that just doesn't happen! Fear of change is a fear of the unknown potential for harm. When every level of the organization is a participant in the change, then ev-

Resistance to change is really resistance to threat. Involve every member of the organization in change and every member increases their sense of control. With control threat disappears.

ery level of the organization owns the change and has control. Control adds predictability which chases away the fear of the unknown and with it, resistance to change. With ownership of change also comes a commitment to the change. Eighty-five percent of change efforts fail because the consultant leaves or leadership changes and things drift back to the way they were. With a simultaneous bottom-up and top-down approach, that can't happen. No one person or one elite group created the change and no one person or elite group benefited from the change. The result was the co-generation of productivity and morale and an increase in engagement at every level of the organization.

The Co-generate System in Action

Advantage Industries, a high technology-based company, used the Co-generate System to create a competitive advantage for its products. They began their change process with the Momentum Triangulated Analysis (MTA). The findings are reflected in the following table:

Triangulated Analysis Key Findings

WEAT *	PDAT**	VBA
• Overall WEAT score in middle of Frequently Unengaged (Green) zone • Organizational Affinity high Frequently Unengaged (Green) zone • Recognition high in Frequently Unengaged (Green) zone • Relationship high in Completely Unengaged (Yellow) zone • Job Match high in Completely Unengaged (Yellow) zone • Growth/Challenge low in Frequently Engaged (Blue) zone • Empowerment high in Completely Unengaged (Yellow) zone	• Co-worker power drain was high in brown-out zone • Supervisor power drain was high in brown-out zone • Resources was low in brown-out zone • Group Dynamic low in Brown-Out • Once resilience was factored in, all other power drains were in the Flicker or lower range	• Independence • Skilled work • Attention to detail *See Appendix I for explanation of Zones of Engagement **See Appendix II for explanation of PDAT zones

The Executive team drew the following conclusions:

• Employees appeared to like the organization and felt the organization valued them. They did not appear to enjoy their jobs and did not feel they had much control over their work.

- Information from the PDAT provided some clues as to why employees might not be enjoying their work. Relationships with each other and their supervisors were not positive and the necessary resources to do their work did not appear to be sufficient. The executive team had recently translated new Federal regulations into a set of practice guidelines that supervisors were instructed to strictly enforce. There had been a lot of complaining that leadership didn't really know what was needed to do the job and the guidelines developed by the executives weren't practical.

- Looking at the top valued behaviors for the organization was a major eye-opener given the incentive-plan the organization had launched a year ago. Employees were given substantial bonuses if they were the top producer in their department. The effect of this program was to emphasize independence and reward quantity over quality. The nature of the work was interdependent so if one person cut corners to compete for the bonus, it would slow the work of others down. This would certainly erode relationships between co-workers and contradicted their valued behaviors of skilled work and attention to detail.

Given these conclusions, the executive team of Advantage Industries did the following:

Organization statregic/cultural level:

In response to the poor relationship indicator, the competitive bonus was eliminated and replaced by a team-based incentive plan that rewarded a combination of quality and quantity.

Group/Work environment level:

In response to the low Empowerment indicator and the high supervisor and resource power-drain, supervisors responsible for meeting Federal standards in the production process were given training in facilitation and advanced listening skills. These supervisors were given the new standards and instructed to meet with their staff to work on developing their own local strategies for meeting these new standards. Once they had their own guidelines, the original guidelines developed by the executive team were removed. Supervisors were also encouraged to gather information from their staff regarding equipment and supply needs.

Individual level:

In response to the low Job Match and Empowerment indicators, all supervisors in the company were trained on how to use the Personal Power Direction Tool and encouraged to teach their employees how to use it. During the yearly evaluation, supervisors were to ask employees how they or the organization could support the individual in executing his or her Personal Power Action Plan.

One year later, Advantage Industries noted the following results:

- When the WEAT* was completed, the overall average score had risen 9 points, moving it from the middle of the Frequently Unengaged (green) zone to the high end of that zone.

- Relationships moved from the middle of the Completely Unengaged (yellow) zone to the middle of the Frequently Unengaged (green) zone. This indicator showed the greatest change of the six indicators.

- Job Match and Empowerment had moved from the high Completely Unengaged (yellow) zone to the middle of the Frequently Unengaged (green) zone.

- Other indicators stayed approximately where they had been the year before.

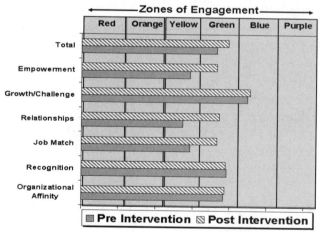

* For a complete discussion of the Zones of Engagement, see Appendix I.

Other positive changes at Advantage were:

- Overall productivity had improved.
- Error rates had been reduced and, with it, losses due to waste.
- Sales had increased in step with the increased availability of high quality product.
- Employee conflict that resulted in disciplinary action had been eliminated.
- Mediations between employees or work groups had been virtually eliminated.
- As a result of implementing Personal Power it was possible to offer more promotions to Advantage staff instead of hiring from outside. There had also been some lateral movement of staff to other positions due to interest or desire to learn.
- Federal standards had been consistently met.

The executive team, supervisors and line staff were all very pleased with the changes that had occurred over the first year. The executive team was surprised at how quickly change had occurred and was even more pleased with how few respondents scored in the "Completely Disengaged" red zone on the latest WEAT. They were now eager to repeat the process and gather the data from the Triangulated Analysis a second time. They would use this data to develop an action plan for the next year so that they could move to an even higher level of engagement.

Skipping the evaluation phase is like studying for a test and then not showing up to take it.

Making a change in the organization's business practices supported the individual line staff in their efforts to build their own work engagement. Correspondingly, increases in individuals' work engagement improved their performance such that their behavioral values of attention to detail and skilled work could be met more easily. The very positive results occurred because each member of the organization had a stake in the change effort. Each member of the organization personally benefited from the changes and the changes touched all parts of the organization.

Evaluating the Change

Once the change momentum has begun, it is important to evaluate the change. This is the step that is most frequently missed for many reasons. Once actions have been implemented, it is often just assumed that they will produce the good they were intended to produce. Sometimes the reason for not doing evaluation is the belief that it is an unjustified expense or that there isn't time for it.

Skipping the evaluation phase is like studying for a test and then not showing up to take it. You may or may not have mastered the material but without the test results, you can only guess. If you have some gaps, you won't know and so you'll never have the opportunity to fill them in. Doing an evaluation after implementing your action plan will allow you to determine whether the actions taken are hitting the mark or whether you need to go back to the drawing board. If your action plan is achieving your intended results, you want to know that so you can avoid unnecessary and counter-productive changes. By the same token, if your action plan is not producing results, it doesn't make sense to continue doing the same thing and expect different results.

If your evaluation indicates that you are not getting closer to your targeted outcomes or the progress toward these outcomes is too slow, one of three things may have happened:

1. your analysis overlooked something or was distracted by some finding,

2. your chosen actions did not match what was needed, or

3. something changed in the environment.

Any of these three situations can easily happen. No matter how objective or unbiased you try to be, your own perceptions and beliefs can color your understanding of the data or your choice of actions. Even with powerful tools, creating change can be messy. The difference is that using a Triangulated Analysis, the degree of messiness and subjectivity is minimized.

Even if you have done an excellent job with the analysis and astutely chosen your actions in response to the data, you can still fall short of your target because things in the environment changed. An irritating or argumentative employee quits and the mix of the work group changes immediately. A large local employer announces massive layoffs and anxiety sweeps through your own workforce. A major supplier goes bankrupt and the switch to another supplier with an inferior product creates havoc with your workers' ability to meet quality specifications. These are just a small sample of the changes you can encounter that will negate or minimize the effectiveness of the actions you are taking to improve work engagement. The evaluation phase of the Co-generate System will allow you to determine whether something critical changed and if so, what changed, how it changed and finally, what actions you should take in response to the change.

The obvious strategy for evaluating the effectiveness of your actions is to do what Advantage Industries did. They did a post-evaluation using the same tools they used for their original Triangulation Analysis. The advantage of this approach is that you are able to compare apples with apples.

Ramona worked for North East Distributors and she did a post-test using the WEAT. She found that the average score for North East Distributors had increased slightly. She was a little disappointed that the increase was not more than it was but she also knew that in the fourteen months between the first and second assessment many things in the office had changed.

Since she had used the MTA to triangulate her data she re-used the tool for her post-intervention evaluation. One of the actions she had implemented was a team-building intervention so she expected to see the Co-worker and Group Dynamic power drain scores to be lower. The results supported that expectation and the *Relationship* indicator of the WEAT also showed a corresponding significant increase. This increase suggested that, much

Measuring the results after implementing change strategies makes continuous improvement and calculating the Return-on-Investment (ROI) possible.

to Ramona's pleasure, the team-building effort had been effective. Changes in the VBA also supported

Ramona's belief that the team-building had been effective because the dominant valued behaviors had shifted a little. "Supportive" now scored higher as a valued behavior than "Efficient."

What Ramona was surprised to see was that the Job Security and Resources power drains were unexpectedly higher than they had been on the previous assessment. These changes were reflected in a slightly lower score in the Organizational Affinity WEAT indicator score. That would explain the small increase in the overall WEAT average score. One indicator had increased significantly but another indicator had decreased!

Ramona recognized that she needed to continue with team-building because it had become *With a post-intervention assessment of engagement, an organization can calculate the value of the change to the bottom-line.* an important valued behavior for the work group. She also realized that she would need to address the change in *Organizational Affinity* with some appropriate action. She examined the VBA for some clues and noticed "Skilled" was still the number one valued behavior. Ramona knew that her department had recently switched to a new technology and the training for it had been slow and of poor quality. Given that "skilled" was a primary valued behavior and that "efficient" was still in the mix, she wondered if the lower job security and resource power drains were related to this change in technology. At her request, a member of the HR department conducted a brief focus group with some of Ramona's staff and the results supported her suspicions. Ramona now knew that if she wanted to improve the *Organiza-tional Affinity* WEAT indicator score, she would need to arrange for better training on the new technology and she would need to reduce anxiety by clarifying her expectations for them while they were adjust-ing to the new technology. Ramona also recognized that any future changes in technology would need to be managed differently than this last change had been managed. With better preparation, a technol-ogy change did not need to erode the *Organizational Affinity* indicator.

By implementing the final phase of the Co-generat-ing System, both Advantage Industries and North East Distributors had put themselves in a position to create continuous improvement. In addition, they were also in a position to calculate the actual value the change intervention had on the company's bot-tom-line.

Valuing the Change

Evaluating the outcomes of actions taken to improve your organization's engagement is an essential com-ponent of the Co-generating System. The whole reason work engagement is important to an organi-zation is because it improves its performance. The challenge is to calculate the return-on-investment the organization obtained as a result of the time and resource invested in improving their average en-gagement level.

Translating changes in work engagement to dollars moves the whole issue from soft fuzzy "feel goods" to hard-nosed, "makes a real difference" actions. It would be nice if employers were committed to making their organization a psychologically healthy place to work because it is the "right thing to do." There are a few exceptions but for most organizations, that just isn't going to happen. Most organizations do not exist to provide work for their employees. Organizations exist to produce targeted results. For-profit organizations must show a profit and not-for-profit organizations must produce their mandated "good."

The good news is that if you improve work engagement, you improve the work environment for the employee AND you also improve the organization's ability to achieve its goals. It's a two-for-one, win-win. Even more, the organization's gain can be measured and quantified into dollars. This can be done in one of two ways. The first way is to use Jack Phillips' (2003) Return-on-Investment (ROI) methodology.

Return-On-Investment (ROI) of a Performance Intervention

The Phillips' model is loosely based on Kirkpatrick's four levels of evaluation (Kirkpatrick, 1987). The first level of evaluation is a measurement of satisfaction with the improvement program. The second level is a determination whether the essential concepts associated with the program have been learned. The third level assesses whether the program is actually being applied in the work setting. It describes what behavior has actually changed. The fourth level determines whether the change has made a positive difference. Findings at each level provides support for the validity of the findings at higher levels. The fifth and final level of the evaluation is the actual ROI. Changes are translated into dollars and compared to the costs of the program. Not all changes measured at the fourth level of the evaluation can be translated into dollars and these Phillips refers to as intangible benefits.

An aspect of Phillips model that adds considerable credibility to the calculation of the ROI is that the effects of the program are isolated. When there is a change in performance, it is quite reasonable that other changes in the organization occurring simultaneously to your performance improvement actions may be responsible for some of the change. Using a variety of tools, Phillips assesses what percentage of the change your efforts can take credit for. This is an important step for both political and validity purposes. Claiming too much credit will not win points with your colleagues who will rightfully believe that their work has also contributed to organizational improvements. Their response is quite likely to attack the validity of your methodology and they will have a case.

If you choose to use this approach, there are a variety of outcome measures you can use, depending on what you have chosen as your targeted action. Phillips provides a list of potential measures that can be easily translated to dollars.

Protecting the good created through implementation of the Co-generating System may depend on being able to translate the value produced into dollars and cents.

Using the Phillips model is an excellent way of translating the benefit of implementing the Co-generate System into bottom-line improvements. It is a conservative approach and uses tools that are familiar to your organization's accountants, which improves its credibility.

Failing to demonstrate that your efforts had a positive effect on your organization's bottom-line is a lost opportunity for career advancement. More importantly this failure can put continued investment in the Co-generating System at jeopardy! Unless the value of higher engagement can be put in dollars and cents, the risk of having your budget cut and wiping out the good created is very real. Using the Phillips methodology, you will be able to produce a defensible estimate of the real contribution improved engagement has made to the organization's bottom-line.

Yearly Improved Engagement Level Dividend (YIELD)

There is another way of determining the value of the change in work engagement. Instead of using the measures suggested by Phillips, this approach calculates the Yearly Improved Engagement Level Dividend (YIELD) factor. The YIELD factor is based on Kravetz's (2004) work calculating the value of improvements in job competencies.

Kravetz's work assumes that if you improve an individual's competency, the value of his or her contribution to the organization also increases. He calculates the value of an increased competency and translates this directly to increased productivity. Productivity in this discussion refers to any increase in volume, timeliness, rate, accuracy, appeal or novelty.

Kravetz's assumption that an increase in a competency translates to an increase in performance is correct if the individual is fully engaged. This individual is working at capacity, given his or her competencies. For the fully engaged, the only way to increase their productivity is to increase their competencies. Below this level, however, a person is not maxing out their current competencies so an increase in a competency just represents an increase in unutilized capacity. It is increases or decreases in work engagement that have the most impact on a person's productivity.

Productivity refers to an increase in volume, timeliness, rate, accuracy, appeal or novelty.

Kravetz argued that the value of an employee's productivity to the employer is at least equal to the cost of employing the person. The cost of employing a person is equal to his wage, plus benefits, plus all the related administrative expenses of providing him or her with work space, equipment, tools, processing his pay, evaluations, training, etc. Kravetz argued that multiplying a person's wage by two is a conservative estimate of the cost to an employer to keep an employee on the payroll.

Using Kravetz' rule of thumb we can calculate the value of the productivity of an employee such as Inez. Since Inez earns \$15 / hour, the value of her productivity to her employer is

$$P = COEx2$$

Where:
P = Value of productivity
COE = Cost of Employment

$30. (P = 2 x COE where COE = cost of employment and P = dollar value of productivity). Using this formula, the dollar value of a change in her work engagement can now be calculated. Inez's raw score on her engagement assessment was 125. A perfect score on this particular version of an engagement assessment is 175. This means an Improvement Gap (IG) of 50 exists. To look at it another way, Inez is performing at approximately 70% of her capacity.

Engagement Score / Maximum Engagement Score
125/175 = .714

For the same cost of employment ($30), it is possible for Inez's employer to enjoy almost 30% more performance from her!

Given that the cost of employing Inez was calculated at $30, and we know Inez's score on her engagement assessment, we can easily calculate the YIELD factor. Inez's employer is currently getting performance from Inez based on 125 units of engagement. Each unit of engagement therefore yields a $499.2 factor.

(COE / Engagement Score) x (40 hrs x 52 weeks)
($30/125) x 2080
.24 X 2080 = $499.60

This YIELD factor means that for every point of engagement, her company is getting 24 cents per hour productivity value. In a 40 hour work week, this is equal to $9.60 and over a year (52 weeks) this is equal to $499.20.
If Inez increases her engage-

YIELD
(COE / Engagement Score) x 2080 hrs.

ment by just one point, her performance to her organization will be worth an additional $499.20 per year. Since Inez's cost of employment remained the same, this is a free benefit to the organization. An increase in work engagement also represents an improvement in quality of life for Inez so both have benefited by this improvement. It should be noted that the YIELD formula assumes an employee is employed fulltime. The number of hours (2080) can easily be adjusted for employees who work parttime.

Given that Gallup (2001a) found that 55% of employees were unengaged, it is not a stretch to believe that half the employees of Inez's organization might be working at about 70% of their capacity, which is the rate calculated for Inez. If there were 100 other employees like Inez and they all improve their engagement score by just one point, the result would be that the organization would enjoy an increase in performance that would result in a $49,920 improvement to the organization's bottom-line! If engagement improved by five points, which is not unreasonable given the Improvement Gap (IG) is fifty points, this would result in $249,600 in increased productivity value. By the same token, losing just five points of engagement would result in $249,600 in lost productivity value. Clearly, increasing work engagement can have a significant impact on the bottom-line of the organization!

Taking this one step further, the YIELD factor does not distribute the gain equally across all levels of engagement. The lower the engagement score, the higher the YIELD factor. That makes sense because the cost of employment remains the same (the numerator) but the number of units of engagement goes down (the denominator).

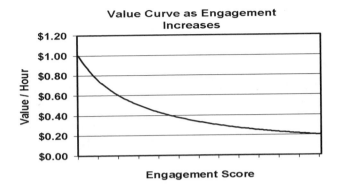

This YIELD factor can be applied to Advantage Industries gain in average engagement to calculate the value of that change to its bottom-line. Advantage Industries total payroll is $1.5 million per year which is equal to $3 million COE. The average engagement score when they started was 115 and they saw a 10 point gain as a result of their efforts.

$3m / 115 = $26,087 per point of engagement
$26,087 x 10 points improvement = $260,870 !

This represents an increase in value but using the Phillips model you can't claim that whole amount because you incurred some expenses to create this increase in value. Using Phillip's fully loaded model for calculating those costs, you will add up the cost of payroll hours involved in producing this change, and every other possible expense that is related to the project. Assuming you estimated the costs at being a very generous $100,000, the increase in the bottom-line you could claim as a result of the engagement project would be $160,870. Phillips equation for calculating ROI is as follows:

$$((Benefit - Cost) / Cost) \times 100.$$
$$((260,870 - 100,000) / 100,000) \times 100 = 160\%$$

That means that for Advantage Industries, the costs of the program are recovered and there is an additional 160% gain. For every dollar they invested in the engagement initiative, they received an additional $1.60. How many investments does an organization make that can offer a return of 160%?

A ten point improvement in engagement resulted in $160,870 improvement in Advantage Industries' bottom-line of the profit and loss statement. When the Advantage Industries profit and loss statement is examined a line item for increased engagement will not be found any more than a line item for improved customer service or quality. However, just as improving customer service or quality has a positive effect on the organization's profitability, so does engagement. What the profit and loss statement will show is a host of improvements in expense control and increased revenues that add up to at least a $161,000. If Advantage Industries showed a profit of $500,000, the ten points of engagement contributed $161,000 to that profit. The engagement initiative would then be responsible for 30% of the organizations' profit.

Full engagement is an unrealistic goal but if the Improvement Gap was 50 points and an increase in engagement of just ten points for 100 employees could produce an increase in bottom-line value of $161,000, how much potential is being lost by this organization? How much potential is being lost by your organization? The most exciting aspect of this is that as the organization is benefiting, and the individual employee is benefiting as well. Work engagement cannot occur without a win-win. Chances of actually realizing full engagement for all employees is unlikely but the target is a worthy one!

With the potential for such significant return on investment, improving engagement should be a priority for any organization. The point of calculating the ROI is to ensure that the cycle of the Co-generating System can be repeated annually, in a continuous improvement loop. Without the ROI, whether you use the Phillips' model or the YIELD, future loops of the Co-generating System could meet the biting edge of budget cuts. The purpose of measuring results should be strictly to inform the next cycle of continuous improvement. In the real world, however, you need to add the ROI to your evaluation so that you can move the Co-generating System out of the "soft fuzzies" and into the world of hard numbers and bottom-line results.

"You can't control what you can't measure."
Tom DeMarco

Chapter *8*

Changing Paradigms

*"Rather than being an interpreter, the scientist who embraces
a new paradigm is like the man wearing inverting lenses."*
Thomas Kuhn

Like Potiphar Breen, many people are sensing that
something significant is occurring all around them.
Something is changing and the familiar rules and
roles aren't working the way they did. Except for the
brave few sensation seekers amongst us, the usual
behavioral response to the unfamiliar is to retreat to
the safety of the known. When we aren't sure what
the right response is under new conditions, we hang
on dearly to the responses that worked for us in the
past.

Unfortunately, hanging on to the familiar, previously safe responses will not work well in the future because the whole lay of the land is changing
too quickly. In the first chapter it was said that "new
challenges require new solutions" and in this new

emerging land old answers are not working.

Covey (2004) says the business world is experiencing a paradigm shift from the industrial to the knowledge economy. Under the industrial economy workers were an expense to be "managed." One worker could be easily replaced by another. The key to success was command and control. *The old industrial economy, based on command and control is being replaced by the knew knowledge-worker paradigm that is built on trust and local control.* Managers made all the decisions and workers did as they were told. A clear hierarchical structure was in place in which orders were given from the top and handed down through the chain of command.

The new paradigm that is emerging is that of the "knowledge worker" who is understood to be an asset, not an expense. With this new paradigm has also come a flatter organization in which the worker is empowered to make decisions. This flat organizational structure is necessary because in this new economy, competitive advantage is earned by those organizations that are able to respond quickly with creative approaches to significant changes. As discussed by Collins (2001) having the right people "on the bus" will make the difference between thriving and just surviving.

Changing demographics in the workforce means the actual numbers of workers available is shrinking and the pool of highly skilled or talented workers is shrinking even faster. Just to fill vacancies, employers need to create "great places to work" because workers choices are increasing daily. The knowledge economy puts an added pressure on the need for good work environments.

Star performers don't remain star performers in unpleasant, unfair or rigid environments. They need and demand to be empowered and to be challenged. Building and maintaining a culture of high engagement is critical to the new economy in which survival will depend on the ability of an organization's workers to apply their knowledge in innovative ways. Organizations will need workers who are able to create new knowledge to deal with previously unknown challenges. Engaged employees will be able to meet the demands of the new economy. Employees constrained by command and control will not be able to.

The old chain of command hierarchical structures build their strength on stability, predictability and uniformity. The new knowledge paradigm demands a flatter structure in which the employee is free to make critical adjustments in real-time. Flexibility and creativity are the keys to success and an engaged workforce is the vehicle that can achieve it.

Paradigms die hard. The truths of a new paradigm make no sense in the context of an old paradigm. Those who have been most successful in the old paradigm will naturally fight the hardest against the new paradigm because

Old paradigms die hard because the truths of the new paradigm make no sense in the context of the old paradigm.

their own personal success tells them the truths of the old paradigm are right. Their success is living proof!

It is not surprising, therefore, that many of the most successful companies of the last fifty years are firmly entrenched in the command and control model. They have complex, multi-layered hierarchies and are steeped in policies and procedures to control every decision. They may sense that things are changing around them and may even adopt some of the language of the new paradigm but it is meaningless and shallow. They may say they value their employees but they cut the labor "expense" by downsizing at the first sign of an economic downturn.

Like Potiphar Breen, organizations caught in the old paradigm may even be tracking the changes around them but their management model prevents them from seeing the pattern that is unfolding. Unable to effectively respond to the changing demands, they work harder at what worked for them in the past. They develop more policies, more procedures, and more rules. They fire talent and go searching for the magic leader who can show them the way while they steadfastly insist on staying on the same path.

Engagement and the Knowledge-Worker Paradigm

Engagement is not equally distributed. In 2001, when Gallup did its survey, only 26% of the workforce scored as engaged. Organizations caught in the industrial paradigm are not getting their

The knowledge worker paradigm naturally builds environments in which full engagement can flourish.

share of the engaged workers. Their work environments are driving their star performers out and into the arms of those organizations who are operating in the new knowledge worker paradigm. This new paradigm understands that it is the ability of the workforce to design new answers, and creatively and quickly respond to new challenges that will keep them in business. The new paradigm respects the worker and recognizes that it must trust its workforce. This new paradigm naturally creates environments in which engagement can flourish. It is able to attract the most talented because these folks understand that they will be able to grow, to learn and to produce in this environment.

If this sounds unrealistic to you or if you find it difficult to believe that such workplaces can and do exist, then perhaps the old paradigm still has a grip on your thinking and your behavior. Epidemic change happens in a predictable pattern. Malcolm Gladwell (2000) described change as beginning slowly, moving from one person to another, gradually building speed until the change reaches a critical mass. When this magic moment of critical mass is reached, the change "tips" and it literally explodes. The change takes on a life of its own as it moves through a population. The gradual change is overtaken by a JOLT.

The paradigm shift toward the knowledge-worker and full engagement is currently well below the tipping point but it is steadily moving toward that tipping point and the JOLT of the new dominant paradigm. Putting one foot in front of the other in the same old path will not get your organization where it needs to be. The question is, will you and your organization be left behind, drowning in the old paradigm? Or will you prepare your organization for the coming JOLT of the paradigm shift?

Change is occurring all around you, do you want to be tossed around by it or do you want to hoist your sails, harness the energy, and make it work for you? Engagement is the means for creating sustainable success in the new economy.

Engagement is the sail that will harness the change energy and help you and your organization navigate the coming JOLT.

References

Adams, J.S. (1963). "Toward an Understanding of Inequity," *Journal of Abnormal and Social Psychology, 67,* 422-436.

American Society for Training & Development (1999). *Trends Watch.* ASTD.

Bandura, A. (1982). "Self-efficacy Mechanism in Human Agency," *American Psychology, 37,* 122-127.

Beck, J.C. and Wade, M. (2004). *Got Game! How the gamer generation is reshaping business forever.* Boston, Mass: Harvard Business School.

Bernthal, Paul. (2004). Measuring Employee Engagement. *Development Dimensions International.* http://www.ddiworld.com

Bernthal, Paul. (2004). E2 and Organizational Outcome. *Development Dimensions International.* http://www.ddiworld.com

Buckingham, M., and Coffman, C. (1999). *First, Break All the Rules: What the world's greatest managers do differently.* NY: Simon and Schuster

Buckingham, M. and Clifton, D.O. (2001). *Now, Discover your Strengths.* NY: Free Press.

Branham, Leigh (2005). *The 7 Hidden Reasons Employees Leave.* NY: AMACOM.

Career Development Services, (2003). "Career Developments," *Newsletter* of Career Development Services, Inc., Sept. 18, 2003.

Cameron, K.S. and Quinn, R.E. (1999). *Diagnosing and Changing Organizational Culture: Based on the Competing Values Frame-Work.* Prentice-Hall.

Clifton, J.K. (2004). *Engaging your employees: Six keys to understanding the new workplace.* www.shrm.org/foundation/engaging.asp

Colias, M. (2004). "Circling the Globe" *HHN Magazine*, November.

Collins, J. (2001). *Good to Great.* NY: Harper

Covey, S. (2004). *The 8th Habit: From Effectiveness to Greatness.* NY: Free Press.

Covey, S. (1990). *The 7 Habits of Highly Successful People.* NY: Free Press.

Crabtree, S. (2004). *"Getting Personal in the Workplace." The Gallup Management Journal*, http://gmj.gallup.com.

Crabtree, S. (2005). "Engagement Keeps the Doctor Away: A happy employee is a healthy employee." *The Gallup Management Journal*, http://gmj.gallup.com.

Daniels, William. (2005). "It's the culture, smarty: Overcoming resistance to performance improvement. *Performance Improvement*, 44(3).

Duxbury, L, Higgins, C., and Johnson, K.L. (1999). "An examination of the implications and costs of work-life conflict in Canada." In L. Duxbury, and C. Higgins, *Work-life balance in the new millennium: Where are we? Where do we need to go?* Ottawa: Canadian Policy Research Networks, Discussion Paper, No. W-12, 2001.

Ellis, A. (1970). *The Essence of Rational Psychotherapy: A comprehensive approach to treatment.* NY: Institute for Rational Living

Gallup (2001a). *"What your disaffected workers cost." The Gallup Management Journal*, http://gmj.gallup.com

Gallup (2001b). *"Gallup study indicates actively disengaged workers cost U.S. hundreds of billions eay year." The Gallup Management Journal*, http://gmj.gallup.com

Gallup (2005). "Unhappy Workers are Unhealthy Too." *The Gallup Management Journal*, http://gmj.gallup.com

Gladwell, M. (2000). *The Tipping Point: How Little Things Can Make a Big Difference.* Little, Brown and Company.

Hammonds, K.H. (2003). "The new face of Global Competition" *Fast Company, Issue 67,* pg. 90.

Harter, J.K. (2001). "Taking Feedback to the Bottom Line." *The Gallup Management Journal,* http://gmj.gallup.com

Herman, R.E., Olivo, T.G., and Gioia, J.L. (2003). *Impending Crisis: Too many jobs, too few people.* Winchester, VA: Oakhill Press.

Herzberg, F., Mausner, B. and Snyderman, B. (1959). *Motivation to Work.* NY: Wiley.

Herzberg, F. (1966). *Work and the Nature of Man.* Cleveland: World.

Human Resources Department, (2002). "Talent Management Emerges as HR Department's New Challenge," *Management Report,* November.

Humber, T. (2003). "Creating a culture of wellness." *Canadian HR Reporter,* v. 21.

Iaffaldeno, M.T. and Muchinsky, M. (1985). "Job Satisfaction and Job Performance: A Meta-Analysis" *Psychological Bulletin, March,* 251-278.

Kirkpatrick, D.L. (1987). "Evaluation" in Craig, R.L. (Ed.). *Training and Development Handbook, 3rd Ed.* Alexandria: American Society of Training and Development, pp. 301-309.

Kotter, J.P. (1973). "The Psychological Contract: Managing the Joining-Up Process," *Management Review,* Spring.

Kowalski, W. (2002). "The Engagement Gap: A growing crisis for Training & Development," *Human Resource Executive Magazine,* December, 2002.

Locke, E.A. & Latham, G.P. (1990). *A Theory of Goal Setting and Task Performance.* Englewood Cliffs, NJ: Prentice-Hall.

Loehr, J. and Schwartz, T. (2005). *The Power of Full Engagement: Managing Energy, Not Time, is the Key to High Performance and Personal Renewal.* Free Press.

Lowe, G. (2002). "Employees' basic value proposition: Strong HR strategies must address work values," *Canadian HR Reporter*, July 15, 2002. www. hrreporter.com

Lowe, G. (2004a). "The Yin and Yang of Change," *Work Environment e-news*, May, 14, 2004. http://www.grahamlowe.ca/newsletter_archive. htm?id=14

Lowe, G. (2004b). *Healthy Workplace Strategies: Creating change and achieving results.* Workplace Health Strategies Bureau, Health Canada.

Lowe, G. (2004c). "Trust Can Ease the Stress," *Globe and Mail*, Sept. 1, 2004.

Management Today (2004). Brain-Food: Masterclass Employee Engagement. *Management Today*, Feb. 05, 2005.

Majumder, S. (2003). "India's 'five-star' hospitals" *BBS News*, 2003/09/29.

Maslow, A.H. (1954). *Motivation and Personality.* NY: Harper & Row.

Maslow, A.H. (1962). *Toward a psychology of being.* NY: Van Nostrand.

McGregor, D. (1960). *The Human Side of Enterprise.* NY: McGraw-Hill.

McLelland, D.S. (1985). *Human Motivation.* Glenview, IL: Scott, Foreman.

Morris, S. (200?). "America's Work Force After the Baby Boomers: The surprising role that immigration will play." *CED in Brief.* Committee for Economic Development.

Pearce, T. (2003). *Leading Out Loud: Inspiring change through authentic communication.* San Francisco: Jossey-Bass.

Phillips, Jack. (2003). *Return on Investment in Training and Performance Improvement Programs*, (2nd Ed.). NY: Butterworth & Heinemann.

Tosti, D., and Amarant, J. (2003). *Energy Investment: Beyond Competence: White Paper.* Vanguard Consulting.

Singh, A. and Datta, M. (2003). "India: First software, now surgery." *Bloomberg News*, March.

Seligman, M.E.P. (1975). *Helplessness: On depression, development and death.* San Francisco, Freeman.

Skinner, B.F. (1969). *Contingencies of Reinforcement.* NY: Appleton-Crofts.

Stein, S.J. and Book, H. E. (2000). *The EQ Edge: Emotional Intelligence and Your Succes.* Toronto, CA: Stoddart Publishing.

Thackray, J. (2001). "Feedback for Real. *The Gallup Management Journal,*" http://gmh.gallup.com

Thorndike, E.L. (1932). *The Fundamentals of Learning.* NY: Teacher's College.

Vroom, V.H. (1964). *Work and Motivation.* NY: Wiley

Wellins, R. and Concleman, J. (2005). Creating a culture for engagement. *Workforce Performance Solutions.* April. pp. 28-25.

Wells, S.J. (2001). "Stepping Carefully: Attention to Staffing Levels, Compensation, and Training Will Help Ride Out a Slowdown," *HR Magazine*, April 19, 2001.

Zemke, R. (1996). "The Corporate Coach," *Training Magazine*, December.

Zemke, Ron, Raines, Claire, and Filipczak, Bob (1999). *Generations at Work: Managing the clash of Veterans, Boomers, Xers and Nexters in your workplace.*

Appendix I

Work Engagement Assessment Tool (WEAT)

The WEAT consists of thirty statements scored on a five-point Likert scale. These statements are divided across the six indicators of engagement discussed in Chapter 3. Scores on the WEAT are divided into six levels or color zones, two zones for disengaged, two zones for unengaged, and two zones for engaged:

Zones of Engagement

Completely Disengaged (Red zone on graph)

> This employee is has completely negative attitude. He or she actively works against the organization, spreading misinformation and distrust. These employees do very little work and the work they do get done is poor. They have already quit their jobs but for a variety of reasons, can't or won't leave. These employees are committed to their negative perception of the organization so there is very little that can be done to improve their performance. The best thing that can happen for these folks is for them to find a way to leave the organization.

Usually Disengaged (Orange zone on graph)

The usually disengaged employee would like for things to be different but doesn't believe that they can be. Most of the time, they are just as negative and unproductive as the completely disengaged employee. Occasionally, if conditions are right, they can muster some energy and be productive for a short time. They cannot sustain it, however, and quickly slip back to their more negative attitude.

Completely Unengaged (Yellow zone on graph)

This employee wants to do a good job but for a number of reasons, is feeling disillusioned, frustrated or blocked. The completely unengaged employee comes to work each day with one major objective and that is to get through the day unnoticed. This employee wants to know the rules and does what absolutely has to be done to keep his or her job. He or she doesn't do anything more. This employee finds it safest to do just what he or she is told.

Frequently Unengaged (Green zone on graph)

The frequently unengaged employee wants to contribute but doesn't trust that the effort will be worth his or her while. This employee is coasting.If conditions are right, however, the frequently unengaged will shift his or her effort up for a short time. When this happens, his or her behavior is more typical of the engaged employee.

Usually Engaged (Blue zone on graph)

Employees that are usually engaged are aligned with the organization. They believe their contribution is valued and their personal goals are aligned with organizational goals. They are energized by their work and take risks by trying creative approaches to problems. The usually engaged employee will question the status quo and advocate for changes they believe to be necessary. They are highly productive and give their best.

Completely Engaged (Purple zone on graph)
Being completely engaged means that the individual is committed to the organization and despite setbacks, doesn't get discouraged. They take risks, are creative problem-solvers and will advocate for changes. Like the usually engaged, they are highly productive and demand excellence of themselves.

> **Zones of
> Engagement**
>
> *Completely Disengaged
> Red Zone
> Usually Disengaged
> Orange Zone
> Completely Unengaged
> Yellow Zone
> Frequently Unengaged
> Green Zone
> Usually Engaged
> Blue Zone
> Completely Engaged
> Purple Zone*

If your organization would like to use the WEAT, it is available at:
http://www.momentumbusinessgroup.com

Appendix II

Power Drain Assessment Tool (PDAT)

The first half of the PDAT consists of one question for each of the common Power Drains discussed in Ch. 4. This assesses the presence and severity of each Power Drain. Questions are scored on a semantic scale:

None
> The issue does not exist.

Flicker
> The issue occurs but it is only brief. It is more of a nuisance, like a buzzing fly, and does not interfere with work. Productivity and morale are affected only briefly, if at all.

Brown-Out
> The issue occurs for longer periods than a flicker and when it does, it is harder to stay focused on work but it **is** possible to continue working. When it occurs it is temporary and usually doesn't last very long. Brown-Out power drains require attention but, provided they are infrequent, they are not urgent. Negative emotions of fear, anger and frustration are aroused by a Brown Out level of a power drain. Both productivity and morale are decreased while dealing with the power drain. It takes some effort to bounce back to previous levels of productivity after contact with a Brown-Out power drain. Morale may return to previous levels if given enough time away from the power drain.

Black–Out
>   When the issue occurs, it affects everything and it is almost impossible to get anything done. It is extremely distracting and upsetting. In a Black-Out, feelings of fear, anger or frustration dominate. If any work is done at all, it is likely to be done poorly because it is a challenge to think clearly when a Black-Out power drain is present. The need to avoid or escape the situation is urgent. Morale is at its lowest point.

Measuring Resilience

Measuring only the presence and severity of Power Drains can be misleading. There may be coping mechanisms, referred to as resilience, in the environment. If the resilience is sufficiently strong, intervention is not be necessary. For that reason, the second part of the PDAT measures the positive energy available in the system for dealing with the issue.

Reslience is measured using a semantic differentiation tool consisting of ten pairs of polar opposite adjectives such as good/bad or fair/unfair. Each power drain has a set of these ten pairs. The pattern of choices amongst these adjectives provides the estimate of resilience. The final score for each power drain reflects the severity with resilience factored in.

A sample of the output of the tool appears below:

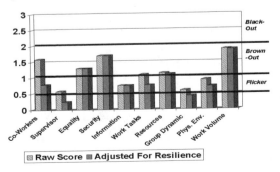

Power drains that score in the Black-Out range after resilience has been factored are urgent. It will be a waste of effort to attempt to build work engagement while a Power Drain in the Black-Out range is present.

Power Drains in the Brown-Out range after resilience has been factored in should be watched. If they don't improve on their own, some effort should be made to change them.

Power Drains scoring in the Flicker zone are very low in priority because they are not strong enough to interfere with efforts to build work engagement. In fact, they will often improve on their own when work engagement improves.

The PDAT provides three sets of data:
   a) the presence and severity of drains;
   b) resilience in the system for coping with the drain; and
   c) a description of the drain based on the frequency of adjective selection.

The combination of these three types of data provides a rich base from which to make decisions. Understanding the strength of a power drain and the degree of resilience for coping with the power drain allows you to accurately prioritize efforts to deal with drains. In addition, the frequency of selection of the various adjectives associated with the drain will give you additional clues regarding what actions will be most effective in addressing the drain. Despite the comprehensive set of data the PDAT makes available, it is a simple assessment that requires less than 10 minutes to complete.

If your organization would like to use the PDAT it can be accessed through http://www.momentumbusinessgroup.com

Appendix III

Adjust and Move Strategies

Examples of Adjust and Move strategies for each of the ten Power Drains.

Difficult Co-Workers	
Adjust	**Move**
• Mediation • Team-building • Contracting • Conflict resolution	• Re-assign to another area or department

Difficult Supervisor	
Adjust	**Move**
• Network with others • Document interactions • Support / join with other coworkers • Conflict resolution • Active listening • Minimize contact	• Transfer to another department

Fairness	
Adjust	**Move**
• Communicate / Educate • Active listening • Negotiation	• Work Audit • Policy development or revision • Procedural change

Scarce Resources	
Adjust	**Move**
• Brainstorm alternative source • Lobby for resources based on cost to organization if resource is unavailable • Collaborate to maximize resources available	• Re-design work to use fewer resources • Add resources

Work Volume	
Adjust	**Move**
• Document work load • Assertiveness training - Saying no • Time management • Prioritize and Delegate	• Re-design job • Add resources

Lack of Job Security	
Adjust	**Move**
• Career development • Communicate • Re-build trust	• Reassign to a less-affected area

Physical Work Space	
Adjust	**Move**
• Modify/correct • Policy development	• Transfer to another area • Remove hazards • Add accommodations

Group Dynamics	
Adjust	**Move**
• Awareness • Mediation • Team-building • Conflict resolution • Guide culture	• Re-assign to another group

Job Tasks	
Adjust	**Move**
• Job re-design • Cross-training • Career development • Empowerment	• Re-assign to another group

Access to Information about Change	
Adjust	**Move**
• Clarify expectations • Communication	• Transfer to a less dynamic area • Policy development

Appendix IV

Ten Avenues for Building Personal Power

1. *Know Yourself*

- Know what your passion is and find a way to do more of it. What excites you? What is it easy to get enthusiastic about? What do you enjoy doing?
- Know what you want to achieve so that you don't get distracted and waste energy chasing the wrong things. If you are good technician and love what you do, a promotion to supervisor might be a disaster.
- Know what you value. Understand what your core values are and make sure that your work aligns with these values. If time at home is important, guard against too much overtime.
- Know your strengths. If you know what you're good at, you can look for ways to use these strengths more frequently. Doing work you are good at builds your confidence and increases your credibility with others.
- Know your weaknesses. There is no need to force a square peg in a round hole. If you know what you don't do well, you can look to find ways to eliminate these tasks from your responsibilities.
- Set goals and a path for yourself. If you can identify what your target is, you can lay out a plan for achieving your goals.
- Anticipate change and prepare for it. Don't get caught unaware. Take time to look down the road. If you know what's coming, it's much easier to cope with it.
- Align your goals with your organization's goals. Complete the Power Boost *Aligning Personal Work Needs and Organizational Goals* exercise (page 103.)

- Identify what your next job will be and prepare yourself for it. Think through exactly what job you would like to have next and then find out what skills and experience will be needed. Begin preparing now.

2. *Remove the Emotional Blocks*

- Challenge your fears, the dangers may be more imagined than real.
- Challenge your myths, we all have them and they can get in our way. See Albert Ellis's Rational Emotive Therapy (Ellis, 1970) for a list of the twelve most common mistaken beliefs.
- Redefine your role. The victim role is a dead-end, even when you really are a victim. Take action.
- Focus on what you can control and let go of the rest. There is only a small percentage of what you are involved in that you really have complete control over. Figure out what it is and work on making a difference in that arena. Accept the rest.
- Allow yourself to try another way – do a short pilot study on yourself!
- Recognize your excuses are actually choices. You are in control of your own choices.
- Re-frame mistakes. Identify what you learned.
- Identify obstacles and develop a plan.

3. *Connect with Others*

- Talk to others. Spend time just chatting. The time isn't wasted. Relationships are important to getting things done and feeling good about your day.
- Find a mentor. Working with a mentor is a short-cut to success. Learning from another's experience means you don't have to start from scratch.
- Network with others. Get to know, at least on a casual basis, as many people as you can. This will increase your opportunities to help others and to be helped by others.
- Accept help from others. You don't have to do it

alone. Two heads are usually better than one and several heads working well together is amazing. Many hands make light work.

- Offer to collaborate with others on important projects. This will give you an opportunity to experience or learn something else and generates gratitude and appreciation, which is always a good thing.

- Let others know what you need or want. People can't read your mind and they would often be willing to give you what you want if they knew you wanted it. Take a chance!

- Brainstorm with others. True brainstorming is a creative process and the more people involved, the more alternatives will surface.

- Greet others. Say hello. It's simple but often overlooked. Take a minute to tour your department. A nod or a comment can change the emotional temperature and will open the door for other needed conversations.

- Talk to strangers. You're a grown up now. Take a chance and talk to at least one stranger a day. It opens the door to serendipity and helps you to feel less isolated.

- Learn and use names. Our names matter to us. When a leader remembers our name, we are impressed and inclined to think well of him or her.

4. Take Action

- Initiate a project. Start something new. A change is often as good as a cure.

- Volunteer for a project. If you hear of a new project, get involved. A new experience or spending time with employees outside of your department will increase your profile.

- Set three small, achievable goals for each day. They can be very simple but you will feel good at the end of the day when you realize you accomplished them.

- Don't wait for permission to make a change. If you

see something that needs to be done, do it and discuss it later. It is often easier to beg for forgiveness than ask permission.

- Set your own standard for excellence and work toward it. Knowing that you have done something as well as you possibly can gives your self-esteem a boost.
- Identify opportunities to use your strengths.People enjoy doing what they are good at so find ways to do more of what you know you are good at. It will boost your self-esteem.
- Look for ways to delegate work that bores you or does not play to your strength. Some of the tasks you hate may be the very thing someone else enjoys.
- Take a risk and see what happens. Failing isn't failing if you learned something along the way. You can't hit a homerun if you won't swing the bat, it's a rule!
- Re-design a process, procedure or task involved in your job. You are an expert in your job, no one knows it as well as you. Find a way to make something simpler or faster and then share it with others.
- Measure something involved in your job and mark your progress. Practice makes us better but we don't always notice. Measure how long it takes you to do something and then measure it again in a month. Chart your improvement.
- Improve your workspace. Hang a picture, get a new stapler or just clean up. Little things can make your work space feel better and increase your sense of control.

5. Re-focus your Thinking
- Meditate. Give your brain a rest and answers to difficult issues will surface.
- Adjust your self-talk. What you think affects your actions.

- Focus on the positive. Positive thinking helps your brain produce the "happy" hormones. You will feel happier.
- Use thought stopping. Block negative thinking and replace it with a positive thought. There are a variety of ways to do this, find the one that works for you by doing some reading on the subject.
- Avoid negative people. Their negative thoughts will infect your thinking.
- Take another perspective. Consider your situation from a supervisor's or employer's vantage point.
- Let go, there's more than one right way. Your way may be great but sometimes it's a lot easier to let someone else lead the way.
- Re-frame the stakes. Re-examine your assumptions about the consequences.
- Dress differently. How you dress affects how you see yourself and how you behave. It also affects how others respond to you. Dress matters. Use it to your advantage.
- Rescue an hour. Find a way to stop doing something or doing less of something.

6. *Improve your Skills*

- Get a degree or certificate. If what you would like to do requires additional credentials, go get them. There may be sources of funding you have overlooked. Talk to a financial counselor at the school, it may be more affordable than you think.
- Attend a workshop, seminar or conference. The right one can get you excited and help you to see new possibilities.
- Read books, journals, newspapers, magazines on a subject or skill area of interest.
- Cross-train. Learn how to do the jobs around you. It will make you more valuable to your organization and help you to see a bigger picture.
- Job shadow. Spend a day in another department to learn what they do.

- Participate in a team project. Working with others will give you an opportunity to see and learn things from other perspectives.
- Know what skills are needed for your next job and begin acquiring them.
- Learn how to respond to job interviews.
- Learn more about your organization. Learn about the history, how things were organized in the past and why things are as they are now.
- Gather information / research. Become an expert, learn something thoroughly.
- Get organized. There are some basic tricks to being organized that you can learn and if you do, you will feel more in control of your day.
- Choose a model and learn from your observations of that model. Watch how someone successful handles stress situations and interacts with others. Notice what works and use it yourself.

7. Help Others

- Teach someone a new skill. Your own skill level will improve when you teach someone else and you will feel good about yourself in the process.
- Mentor a new or junior employee. Help a new or junior employee to benefit from your experience. It feels great.
- Pitch in. Helping others feels good, builds relationships and increases learning.
- Volunteer in your community. It can help put more purpose in your life and you may bump into important experiences or opportunities.
- Let others know what you see as their strengths. Give others the praise you would like and it will come back. More then that, you will improve your relationships and encourage others development.
- Give others the benefit of the doubt when considering motives for their behavior. Jumping to conclusions regarding peoples reasons for doing things can lead you down an unproductive road.
- Plan a celebration for people's birthdays or retire-

ments.
- Acknowledge the success of others. Let others know you noticed. Help others see their accomplishments. People don't usually give themselves credit for what they do.
- Be a friend. Relationships make the work more pleasant, or at least more tolerable.
- Take advantage of opportunities to do favors for others. People find it hard to be critical of people who do nice things for them.
- Bring a treat. Home baked cookies can change a mood!

8. Get Healthy
- Exercise. You'll feel better and think better.
- Sleep. Get more rest and you will feel less depressed and more in control.
- Drink more water. The benefits of good hydration on the body has a range of positive effects.
- Eat better. Give your body the right energy to operate on.
- Control caffeine and smoking.
- Watch less T.V. (Especially the crime or violent shows. They contribute to fear and anxiety.)
- Introduce stress management strategies. Explore the alternatives and find one that works for you.
- Balance work / family / play.
- Breathe deeply. Increasing oxygen in the body will clear your mind.
- Pause and count backwards from 100. Give your brain a short rest!
- Smile. It will trick your brain into thinking you're happy and it will produce more of the "happy" hormones.
- Keep a journal to sort out your feelings over time.
- Take a walk. It combines the benefits of exercise and meditation. You can have two for the price of one!

9. Reward Yourself

- Take time to enjoy. You can miss the best things if you don't slow down.
- Count your blessings. Grandma was right. Counting your blessings will remind you of what is going right and the things in your life that really matter.
- Budget time for fun. All work and no play makes Jack a dull boy. It also compromises the quality of Jack's work. Take time for yourself.
- Add laughter. It increases your oxygen and helps your brain produce more of those "happy" hormones.
- Notice your own accomplishments. Give yourself credit! Praise yourself. It's easy to be self-critical. It's harder to praise yourself.
- Forgive yourself. Learn from a mistake and then let it go. You can't undo it so don't let it interfere with your ability to do it better the next time.
- Promise yourself treats. Help yourself meet goals by rewarding yourself.
- Take pride in what you do. Understand its purpose.
- Keep toys in your office. Little distractions can help you give your brain a rest.

10. Be Clear

- Learn to be more assertive. It's not the same as being aggressive.
- Learn to listen. There is tremendous power in being able to really listen.
- Ask for what you want. Others can't read your mind. Let people know.
- Learn the tools for influence. There are eight tools that are based on psychological principles. Make them work for you or they may be working against you.
- Learn how to ask effective, non-threatening questions. The right question can elicit critical information.

- Learn how to tell an effective story. People are more likely to understand an issue when they can relate to a story.
- Learn how to give persuasive oral presentations. You can be more successful if you use the right model.
- Improve your ability to negotiate with others. Logic and data are rarely enough to resolve an issue when emotions get mixed in. Learn the tools for getting past barriers.
- Demonstrate appreciation of others' contributions.
- Build trusting relationships with others. If you promise something, follow through.
- Clarify your expectations. Don't assume that others understand what results you want. Take the time to explain.
- Get clarification of others' expectations. Don't assume that you know what others want. Check it out and get clear information.
- Talk to someone outside your immediate work group. Get past your organizational silos and see things from other perspectives.
- Communicate face-to-face whenever possible. Email and text messages are wonderful but without the voice tone and non-verbal gestures, you can make the wrong assumptions. The same thing said with a slightly different voice inflection can change its meaning dramatically.
- Explain your reasons for decisions. Help people to understand how you arrived at your decision. It may help them to accept it.
- Find out first-hand why a decision was made. There may be information that influenced the decision that you didn't have. It may be easier to accept the decision when you understand why.